Cutting My Own Path
The Guy Wyser-Pratte Story

By
Guy P. Wyser-Pratte

Published by E&R Publishers
New York, NY, USA

An imprint of MillsiCo Publishing, USA
www.EandR.pub

Copyright: © 2025 Guy Wyser-Pratte—All rights reserved.

Except for brief quotations in critical articles or reviews, no part of this book may be reproduced in any manner without prior written permission from the publisher. Write to: Permissions, Publisher name, E&R Publishers, New York, NY, USA.

ISBN: 9781966155140-Hardcover
ISBN: 9781966155188 Jacketed Hardcover
ISBN: 9781966155157 Softcover
ISBN: 9781966155164-Ebook
ISBN: 9781966155171-Audiobook

Library of Congress Control Number: 2025936100

DEDICATION

To those who refuse to follow the script

To the risk-takers, rule-breakers, and the ones who dare to carve their way.

To my family, who gave me roots, and to my mentors, who gave me wings.

To the moments of near defeat that taught me resilience, and the victories that proved it was all worth it.

And to the next generation—may you never be afraid to take the road no one else sees.

This book is for you.

Guy

CONTENTS

Foreword vii
1. My Idyllic Beginning 1
2. The Great Escape 5
3. New Horizons 7
4. The Beckoning of the Military 11
5. Angels and Aprons 17
6. Storms, Secrets, and a Woman With a Knife 19
7. From a USMC Infantry Officer to Global Finance 25
8. Risk Arbitrage—What It Is and Why I Opened It Up to Wall St 31
9. Bache & Company 37
10. The Arc of The Arbitrage Industry 43
11. Arbitrage to Activism—My Journey Begins 55
12. Prudential-Bache—A Tale as Old as Time 69
13. The Activist Awakens 77
14. Friendly Persuasion—A New Arrow in My Quiver 81
15. The Many Faces of Activism 89
16. Brothers in Arms 101
17. Sticking to Your Knitting 103
18. The Name on the Door—The Resurrection of Wyser-Pratte & Co. . . . 107
19. Courts, Cultures, and Close Calls 115
20. Family, Legacy, and the Soft Side of a Street Fighter 121
21. My Remaining Summers 125
Letter To My Younger Self—Epilogue 129

At any time, Scan the code below to view the related image gallery in full color or visit www.Cutting

FOREWORD

BY BRIGADIER GENERAL THOMAS V. DRAUDE—UNITED STATES MARINE CORPS (RET)

There are men who follow the rules, and there are men who rewrite them. Guy Wyser-Pratte has never been interested in the former.

I first came to know Guy not through headlines or boardroom battles—but through his steadfast commitment to the Marine Corps. Long after hanging up his uniform, Guy poured his heart, his mind, and his formidable Rolodex into strengthening the intellectual foundation of our institution. As President, Vice Chairman, and Chairman of the Marine Corps University Foundation, he didn't just raise funds—he raised standards. He believed that strategic thinking should be as much a part of a Marine's toolkit as a rifle. He understood that Foundations exist to "Change lives and to save lives." Both were achieved under his leadership.

But as you'll soon discover in these pages, Guy's influence stretches far beyond Quantico or Wall Street.

He is, at his core, a fighter. Born into chaos on the beaches of wartime France, he cheated death more than once before his sixth birthday. He served with distinction in the United States Marine Corps, navigating the shadows of the Cold War, and the jungles of Southeast Asia. And when he entered the world of high finance, he carried the same code of Honor, Courage, and Commitment—core values of the Marine Corps—the code that defined his military career.

You'll read about boardroom showdowns that would make Hollywood screenwriters blush. About legal battles that spanned oceans. About narrow escapes—both literal and metaphorical—that tested the limits of luck, grit, and instinct. You'll also read about betrayal, family, loss, and the hard-earned wisdom that only comes from going 10 rounds with life, and getting up for the 11th.

What separates Guy from the rest isn't just his intellect or success. It's his refusal to compromise what he believes in. Whether fighting for shareholder rights, the soul of the Marine Corps, or his own survival, he never backed down from a righteous cause. And he never, ever settled for the easy path.

This is not a sanitized tale of success. It's the unfiltered account of a man who lived on his own terms—sharp-edged, principled, and fully aware that choosing the unbeaten path means you often walk it alone.

If you're looking for inspiration, you'll find it here. If you're looking for a life measured not by titles or trophies, but by impact, resilience, and defiance—look no further.

Semper Fidelis,

Brigadier General Thomas V. Draude

---

*Gen. Draude executed one of the greatest deceptions in military history during Desert Storm. His then title was 1st MEF (Marine Expeditionary Force) Deception Officer. He had Marines circling offshore Kuwait in landing craft, as they normally do in preparation for an amphibious landing. All of Sadam's artillery was pointed out to sea. In the meantime, a Brigade which included the XVIII Airborne Corps, the 1st Cavalry Division, the 1st Marine Division, and allied Arab, British, and French forces crept up behind Sadam's forces, overwhelming them and forcing Sadam's retreat to Bagdad. My buddy Tom Draude! His distinguished career included 3 tours in Vietnam.

1. MY IDYLLIC BEGINNING

As the gentle spring sun streamed down softly, warming my Austro-Hungarian skin, I sat in stupefied wonder and contentment. Had I been older than two years, I may have been aware that I was sitting in the very middle of World War II. But for me—laying back in my diaper-clad nirvana on a pristine beach in Cannes, France—I was duly enamored with my existence thus far.

I began my journey two years earlier on June 21, 1940. My mother—an Austrian Catholic—was from Gratz in the east of Austria, which was a very staunchly conservative part of the country where the Hitler Youth was very prominent. My mother's brother, Tony, was a member of the Hitler Youth and became a colonel in the Waffen SS—a combat branch of the Nazi Party's paramilitary Schutzstaffel (SS) organization.

He was an Obersturmbannführer—a paramilitary rank in the German Nazi Party that was used by the Sturmabteilung (SA)—roughly translating to Storm Troopers—and the SS. You can imagine that the family on both sides was none too pleased when my mother met and agreed to marry my Hungarian Jewish father. Both sides were throwing boulders at them.

My grandfather, Baron Anton Prattès, was a very close friend of Kaiser Franz Joseph. The Kaiser not only they gave him the title of Baron but also appointed him as Hofrat—the court counselor or consigliere as the Italians say. They would often hunt together so my grandfather would have the excuse of it being work related but when other needs arose, and the Kaiser wanted to be with his mistress, a more strategic role manifested, that of beard.

Ah, the richness and diversity of the family tree. Of course, the Baron was none too pleased about his putative Hungarian-Jew son in law. I am sure fits were thrown.

My mother was soon expecting me in the spring of 1940. The family lived in a chic apartment on the Avenue Émile Deschanel, on the Champs de Mars, right smack next to the Eiffel Tower. War hadn't broken out in France quite yet, but the Germans were on their way, and through the Ardennes Forest—a region in southeast Belgium that extends into Luxembourg, Germany, and

France—rolled Uncle Tony as part of General Guderian's Panzer division "en route" to take over Paris, and Uncle Tony knew where we lived. He had been there before the war broke out.

My mother knew Tony was approaching and did not wish to give birth to a child anywhere near her Nazi brother. Thus, my father and mother decided to move us to Vichy. Of course, Vichy then became the head of "occupied France" when Maréchal Philippe Pétain signed the armistice agreement with Adolf Hitler—in the same train car and location, incidentally, as the 1918 armistice signing in Compiegne, France. History doth repeat, as the saying goes. When Pétain signed the armistice on the 22nd of June 1940, he started making the rounds of the hospitals and embracing the newborns. I feel compelled to note that I had the peculiar distinction of being one of those babies!

The government was presided over by Maréchal Pétain, who was known as the "hero of Verdun" from the World War I battle that inflicted 337,231 French casualties. The Germans took 330,000, but the French Army had survived. Pétain was probably a little too old to take that responsibility and didn't quite know what he was getting into, but he did save France from total destruction; I will give that credit to him.

So, we moved to Vichy, which was now "occupied France." The South was still considered "unoccupied." My father was being sought by the Nazis because he was not only Jewish, but he was also an unofficial adviser to the socialist prime minister of France named Léon Blum. My dad, naturally, thought he was smarter than the Germans, so he kept moving us from one place to the next in France. Vichy to Cannes was just the beginning, as Cannes was still part of "unoccupied" France. We lived there for a year or two. My mother—with the heart of a warrior—had to defend her family a number of times when German officers would come to our villa and want to occupy it. She would aggressively send them on their way like errant schoolboys, saluting and marching off after she got through with them in their own dialect.

When the Allies landed in French North Africa on November 8, 1942, "unoccupied" became "occupied" France, so it was time to move from Cannes to a safer area. Additionally, things were getting a little bit too hot for my father, so he relocated us to a town in the Haute-Savoie department, located in the Auvergne-Rhône-Alpes region of Southeastern France. We settled in Menthon-Saint-Bernard, a beautiful area on the Lac d'Annecy, a bucolic lake haven.

We rented a villa there, la Villa les Presles, living in seemingly quiet tranquility. My fondest memories were of me and my dad, hand in hand at age 2, going to the bakery (boulangerie) to buy our morning baguette.

In front of and behind us on the baguette line stood Nazi officers in their black uniforms. If they only knew! It now reminds me of Paul Newman in the star role in the film *Exodus*—who was Jewish in life, as an Israeli dressed in a British officer's uniform—being told by his commanding officer that he could smell a Jew a mile away. Really?

On the way home, my dad would routinely break off the end of my pre-breakfast. By the time we got home, half the loaf had been devoured.

All this came crashing to an end when the Allies landed in French North Africa (Operation Torch) on November 8, 1942, and Southern France quickly became part of "occupied France." Well, time to skedaddle, pack up, and head for the area of the Haute-Savoie on the Swiss border, renting la Villa les Presles in Menthon-Saint-Bernard, bordering not only the beautiful Lac d'Annecy but, not coincidentally, the Swiss border. There we lived in relative obscurity, each of the three boys with very Catholic names: Jean Michel (St. Michael), Guy Patrick (St. Patrick), and Yves Christian Bernard (St. Bernard), the youngest, born there on Valentine's Day in 1944. My dad had prepared well for what must have seemed to him a rapidly approaching necessity. He made friends with a Swiss border guard and made several trips into Switzerland with the border guard's help, each time paying him in gold Krugerrands. I can only assume that this was the guard, one of the "angels on my shoulder," who would save my life. Speaking of angels, another appeared on my shoulder in the form of the local curé, Père Chamosset who—seeing the imminent danger—changed my 2 year old baptismal certificate from Guy P. Weiser to Guy P. Wyser. When Chris was born, he extended the same favor to him, at great risk to himself. Chris visits his grave on his every visit to Menthon-Saint-Bernard. Père Chamosset was the first of many angels.

2. THE GREAT ESCAPE

In an event that evokes shades of Steve McQueen's famous motorcycle jaunt in escaping the German POW camp, my father received word that somebody from a nearby commune—Talloires—had turned him in to the police. The "police"—otherwise known as the ruthless Milices (militias), run by the notorious Pierre Laval—were mandated to send French Jews to Drancy and from there to the concentration camps. My father—having been tipped off to this act of a Judas—quickly decided that it was time for the family to cross the border into Switzerland. The Swiss border was not far from the house, which I am sure was orchestrated purposefully by my father.

To me it was a grand adventure—until it wasn't. As we made our way to the border, I began to get the sense that my mother was ill at ease. As we neared our crossover point at the border fence, I could feel the intensity of our circumstances become apparent. To get across, we had to climb through a hole in the fence. It was the only way to avoid the other guards patrolling the perimeter of the fence. My father was to go through first to test the passage. To do so, he hid in an open grave at night until the guards were at the farthest point from him. He scrambled through to safety. The next day, my mother, her three sons, and three nannies were instructed to go across the same place in the fence in broad daylight. I was the last one through the hole in the fence, and I was about halfway through when suddenly I heard the galloping sound of a horse behind me. Out of bewilderingly stupid curiosity, I took it upon myself to go and see what it was all about, so I went back through the hole in the fence into France to be confronted almost immediately by a German officer on horseback. Seeing me, he immediately figured out what I was doing and pulled his weapon out of his holster. Putting my hands over my eyes, I heard the shot. I was sure I was dead. In petrified shock I uncovered my eyes to see that there was nobody on the horse. Behind him, also holding his gun, was a Swiss guard, who was not about to see a five-year-old get put away by the Nazis. My mother grabbed me and was so angry that for one moment I thought I was almost in more danger from her than the Nazi. She broke an umbrella over my skull, knocked me unconscious, and pulled me to safety on the Swiss side.

From there, we went and lived in a camp in Switzerland for several months until the war was over. We soon moved back to France and lived in a city called Sèvres, which is a French commune in the southwestern suburbs of Paris and makes very beautiful, world-famous porcelain. But this was not destined to be our long-term home.

Thirty-five years ago, I went back to Menthon-Saint-Bernard to visit the Villa "Les Presles." I knocked on the door, and a lovely lady, Madame H. De Germond-Stubli, answered, greeting me with, "I know who you are, your mother and father visited here with me a few years ago. Your mother was so elegant. She wore white gloves." She gave me her visit card, which I still carry as one of my cherished belongings. Of course, we reminisced about our past history, to my great appreciation of what the area had experienced under Nazi control. I had my daughter Joëlle visit her while on an exchange program from Tufts University. The villa still stands and holds precious memories for me.

3. NEW HORIZONS

Life was not unkind in Sèvres but my father at this point had grown weary of being at the hands of the Germans both in World War I and now World War II, and had visions of Russian communists taking over France as they were occupying many countries in Eastern and Central Europe. So he decided it was time to move the family to somewhere far, far away. We had been in Sèvres for a year, but in March 1946 it was time to emigrate.

My father had a special visa from the US Treasury Department because—by the end of the war—he had begun importing condensed milk for children into France. In wartime, milk was not readily available. I can remember to this day the sweet, beautiful taste of the Nestlé Condensed Milk. To facilitate the importation of the product, my father had to provide the funds to finance the milk imports. The only way to reclaim it from the Treasury Department was to go there—to Washington, D.C.—in person. This was the catalyst that inspired this bold move to board a ship and come to a new world. The United States of America. On a vacation, we were told.

My father booked us on a troop ship to come to America. The ship was called the USS *Hood Victory*, departing from Le Havre on March 1, 1946. (My granddaughter Louisa, as a school research project, found the ship's manifest and gave it to me for my birthday. It hangs proudly in my study.)

All these GIs aboard our ship were coming back from the war. Somehow my father was able to get us passage. On the way, I remember, we ran into terrible seas. I think that's where I first gained the ability to not be seasick. Everybody else got horribly seasick. It was so bad that I remember going up to the ship's hold, and at the middle of the ship all the troops were gathered around trying to stabilize the ship. That storm was really bad, but the troops did a pretty good job of stabilizing it.

Eventually, we landed at Ellis Island, where we were to be screened for entry into the United States. Of course, my father had the appropriate papers from the US Treasury Department to gain access, so we went through there in pretty short order and came out onto the docks in lower Manhattan in March of 1946. We took a taxi and started to roll up First Avenue.

My father was taking us to the Hotel St Moritz, where he had booked rooms for us, and I noticed that there were all these people on the street drinking and having a great time all the way up First Avenue. I said to my father, "What a great country this is, everyone is just out celebrating." "You idiot," my father barked at me while smiling, "It's Saint Patrick's Day." We stayed at the St Moritz—now known as the Ritz-Carlton on Central Park South—for three months on our "vacation," and after three months, my father came home one day and said, "I bought a house!" To which I said, "Really? What about all my friends and my toys in France?" "Forget it," said dad. "We're staying in America."

The house that he bought was in Jamaica Estates, Queens, which, incidentally, was also the first home of the current president. Make of that what you will. My first school was a Catholic school named the Sacred Heart Academy on Midland Parkway, which is right on the same street as where our house was located, so I walked to school every day. After about four years of hearing about how life was just a bunch of sins for which we needed to seek salvation, I'd just about had enough of the nuns. My father moved us to a large manor house in Pelham Manor, thanks to a windfall profit he made on speculating against the British pound in 1950. My new school was Iona Preparatory in New Rochelle, in Westchester County. I was there through grammar school and then high school. The school was run by the Irish Christian Brothers, who were a bunch of right-wing fanatics, but the school did me well enough. I was on my way. While at Iona, I learned to play baseball and began an ice hockey career on the local lakes as soon as they froze—sometimes even before they were completely frozen!

In New Rochelle, we lived near the Thomas Paine cottage on Broadview Avenue. Thomas Paine is so important in American history because he was the one who wrote the book *Common Sense*, which was calling for America—still a British colony—to revolt against the British government. His famous quote, "These are the times that try men's souls," rings to this day.

I recall I used to go running across people's back lawns to get to school in the morning, and as I look back, having read the book by John Cheever called *The Swimmer*, it reminded me of hopping from one person's property to the next, all in their backyards, enjoying the scenery until I reached the baseball field behind the school, my own "field of dreams."

When I got tired of my newspaper delivery career, I joined the Civil Defense Corps at age 15, setting atop New Rochelle Hospital with a direct line to a government operator, in order to report any airplanes flying within sight. It was the period of the scary fifties, when kids were taught to hide under their desks in case of a nuclear attack. I think this stood me in good stead for my later activities as from early in the 2000's until 2024 I would come to work under contract with the CIA. I obviously can't reveal my activities, but I am proud of this additional layer of patriotism to my adopted country. My older brother would also work for them, but in their "special ops." Choppers would hover over his house in order to whisk him away on missions. But for now, back to my earlier days.

My family's story in America is etched not only in memories but also in paperwork. I still have my parents' applications for French citizenship and, later, their naturalization documents for American citizenship. One detail that always stood out to me was how intentional they were about our name—how it reflected their journey and identity.

My father's last name was originally Weiser—a name that clearly revealed Jewish heritage. At one point, my mother said, "We can't go around the States with Weiser. It's too obvious." So, my father shortened it to Wyser—hence his first company: E. Wyser & Company.

When we became American citizens in August 1952, we had the opportunity to make a more significant change. My mother's maiden name was Prattès—with an "s" at the end, distinctly Austrian. My father suggested combining the two names into Wyser-Pratte—hyphenated, like many European families do to mark something meaningful. For us, that moment was about becoming Americans, and my father converting to Catholicism. I think he felt he owed it to my mother, who had saved us all on numerous occasions.

But there was a moment of hesitation. My mother said, "Why don't we just drop the Wyser and go with Pratte?" My father's reply was firm: "Hell no." He was immensely proud of his name and heritage, and he wasn't going to erase that part of himself.

So, for Wyser-Pratte, it became a symbol not just of heritage but of transformation and belonging in a new country. I still have all the court documents showing the legal name change, as well as my naturalization papers. Some of the original records were lost in the shuffle at the State Department, but I may apply to get a new copy one day. It's more than paper—it's proof of the road we traveled to become who we are.

4. THE BECKONING OF THE MILITARY

Next, I set my sights on successfully competing for and obtaining an NROTC scholarship, which serves as an augmentation to the US Naval Academy. I chose to use the scholarship at R.P.I., a hockey power in the East, but there was "no room for me at the inn." I returned to visit Navy Commander Forebush, who had selected me for the scholarship, and the latter helped me get assigned to the University of Rochester, where I happily matriculated for four years. The Irish Christian Brothers at Iona refused to give me a recommendation there—despite my 1958 Class Valedictorian status—because it was a non-Catholic university, so I took the diplomatic path and said, "Screw them and their recommendation," and went to the University of Rochester for four wonderful years. It was there that I joined the prestigious fraternity Theta Chi. I also became social chairman of the fraternity and of my class. Golden years indeed.

My initial studies were involved in mechanical engineering, in which I lasted exactly one week. I recall my first mechanical drawing class; after moments of careful consideration, I said, "This is not for me," and that was that. I knew that the University of Rochester had a terrific history department, so I switched over into the humanities and majored in American diplomatic history, which enabled me to follow the antics of America's presidents in grabbing control of various parts of the United States. I was particularly interested in the Monroe Doctrine, a cornerstone of US foreign policy, declared in 1823, which stated that the Western Hemisphere was no longer open to European colonization and that any interference in the affairs of the Americas by European powers would be viewed as a hostile act against the United States. I wonder to myself these days if the Monroe Doctrine may have been consulted in the naming of the suspiciously expansionist "Gulf of America," but I'll reserve judgment on such things.

As a freshman, I decided that my high school ice hockey days ended prematurely, but an ice hockey team is something that the University of Rochester was sadly lacking. So, naturally, in a somewhat self-serving move, I started an ice hockey team there, eventually becoming its captain, and lo and behold, more than 60 years later, it's still a thriving ice hockey team. I noticed they don't invite me back to play too much these days. Back when I started the team, I got a grant from the university's athletic department to buy uniforms and whatnot, and we went off and played all the local teams. I had a merry old time getting up at five in the morning to practice on an outdoor rink across the Genesee River, freezing our butts off, but nonetheless getting in a good hour and a half of skating every day—so much so that by the time I got to my 8 o'clock class, I promptly fell asleep.

Ice hockey played a meaningful role in my early life—an arena of pride, camaraderie, and, occasionally, humility. From my freshman year through graduation at the U of R, I was part of a team that gave me a deep sense of belonging. We weren't the most elite group, but we had heart, and we played with passion. I took great pride in outskating the opposition. It was one of the most rewarding team experiences of my youth.

But once I joined the Marine Corps, hockey was over. There are no ice rinks in the Corps, and I had to let it go. I would've loved to continue playing, but there was simply no way.

There's one hockey story that's stayed with me—one of those humbling, self-deprecating memories that I've never really lived down. We had scheduled a game against Cornell. At the time, we were still a junior team, and I had personally arranged the match. Cornell, meanwhile, had all these kids imported from Welland, Canada, who skated like the wind. And lo and behold, they had none other than Ken Dryden in the nets, who later led the Montreal Canadiens to several Stanley Cup championships.

Before every game, I'd head across the Genesee River to a local guy who sharpened skates. On this occasion, though, he botched the job—whether from laziness or too much to drink, I'll never know. Instead of sharpening both sides evenly to create a balanced edge, he did just one side. I had no idea until I stepped onto the ice.

I was the captain of the team, and the minute I got out there, I started falling all over the place. I couldn't skate. Embarrassed beyond words, I pulled myself from the game—I couldn't do that to my team. We were slaughtered by the Cornell guys; they skated circles around us. I still have nightmares about it. To this day, I can picture myself on that ice, legs flailing, and hear myself thinking, I can't skate. Oh my God.

As a Naval Reserve Officers Training Corps (NROTC) student, I had the most marvelous experience because every NROTC university had a major or lieutenant colonel from the Marine Corps who took care of the Marine Option students. I was the only Marine Option student as a junior, so it was just Major Victor Ohanesian and me in the class. The major drove me very hard to be the best NROTC student on the U of R campus. What a strapping specimen of a man he was. He was killed in Vietnam, bleeding out at a time when a shrapnel wound needed speedy medical help, which simply couldn't reach him in time. I came back to the university to deliver his commemoration speech in 1995.

In your junior year at university, you had to decide whether you wanted to stay in the US Navy or join the Marines. So I decided, since I already had a brother who was a Marine officer, I would follow in his footsteps. I wasted no time in fully embracing life as a Marine Option student, and I won all the drilling competitions. I embraced life so passionately that they made me the Commander of the Corps of Midshipmen in my senior year. There is a photo in the web gallery showing the Corps.

When you're officially a Marine Option student, they send you to Quantico, Virginia, for six weeks to get the hell kicked out of you. It is called your "Bulldog Summer". The drill instructors and teachers are from Paris Island, which is where the East Coast enlisted Marines get to train. These drill instructors train their future officers, and let me tell you, they don't hold back. If you are ever wondering who you truly are, if you don't find it there, you never will. I knew that it was going to be hell, so I bought myself a pair of combat boots and would run 5 miles a night for weeks in preparation. By the time I got down to Quantico, I was in better shape than anybody down there. I remember these big football players lying aside these hills that we had to run up and down, standing there with oxygen, but I was so well prepped I breezed it in.

Before Quantico, one goes every summer on a six-week cruise with the US Navy as a "midshipman." For my first-year cruise, I was on what they called Operation Inland Seas, during which we followed Her Majesty's Royal Yacht *Britannia* to ceremoniously open up the St Lawrence Seaway—a waterway connecting the Atlantic Ocean to the Great Lakes—and it was a blast of a cruise because, for the most part, all we mostly did was wear our white dress uniforms and have debutante balls wherever we went, while the Marines aboard our fleet practiced amphibious landings. Imagine Marines landing on the shores of Chicago, which they did there and in key cities of the Great Lakes.

I had learned some very important things in the navy, and one of them was you do not want to be a supernumerary in the engine room. That was a piece of naval service that I was very pleased to leave behind. Marines were, as far as I was concerned, all about being on the land. It was about a six-week cruise, and we went all the way to Lake Huron up through the canals, locks, and so forth. I spent the better part of a year at sea—but above decks!

This first cruise was on a big old heavy World War II cruiser called the USS *Macon*. When I say we smashed our way through the Eisenhower locks, I mean we literally smashed them going through. The second cruise I was on, we spent three weeks at Little Creek, Virginia, with the Marines learning about amphibious warfare, amphibious landings, and such. Up and down ships and nets, crawling around, it was an entire adventure on its own, but the last three weeks of that second summer were in Corpus Christi, Texas, where they try to entice you into becoming a naval aviator. Well, after I threw up in a cockpit a few times doing barrel rolls with some hotshot pilot hell-bent on setting me straight—who made me clean out my cockpit—I decided that being an aviator was also not for me. After all that, Quantico was light work. For me, at least.

And after all that, you graduate, get officially commissioned, and they send you right off to basic school, which was supposed to be a nine-month training as an infantry officer, but because of the Cuban Missile Crisis, they cut it to six months and sent us right out to the fleet. They asked me where I wanted to go, and I said immediately, "The Far East." I knew that there was a police action going on in the Republic of South Vietnam. I thought that maybe that was the way I could get into some action. I tried hard as a young man, full of piss and vinegar, to go and get into trouble, by which I mean getting involved in some combat action. I wound up with a great outfit, which was the Third Reconnaissance Battalion of the Third Marine Division, where we reconnoitered beaches and all kinds of mischief. Sometimes we operated out of submarines, launching in little rubber boats at night and being pulled into shore by the periscope of the submarine. It was a wonderful experience.

Upon arriving in Okinawa, I was informed that the only major operation underway was a so-called police action in the Republic of Vietnam. I remember thinking, well, that's good enough for me.

After about six months serving as a platoon commander—with one photo capturing me and three fellow platoon commanders of "Charley" company from that time—I was offered the opportunity to join a mission to South Vietnam. They called it "on-the-job training" (OJT). The plan was to patrol with South Vietnamese Marines around the Strategic Hamlets, where the Viet Cong were terrorizing local civilians. The American strategy, under Ambassador Henry Cabot Lodge, was to relocate villagers to a secure location and to isolate them from the Viet Cong. I was selected to be an advisor for one of the Vietnamese battalions. I was enthusiastic about the mission. I could speak French, which I hoped would be useful with the South Vietnamese officers. But just a day before departure, I was asked to produce my American passport, required at that time for travel and access to Vietnam during the advisory phase of the war, under the Military Assistance Command Vietnam (MACV). Unfortunately, I didn't have one.

As it turned out, I hadn't been born in the United States and thus needed my naturalization papers to apply for a passport. I called my parents, who understood the gravity of the situation and, like any worried parents might, delayed sending the documents. I sped down to Naha, where the American Consulate was located. I begged the consul, Anne Pomeroy, to make an exception and grant me a passport. Just before my stateside papers arrived, I received a telegram from the Commander of the Pacific Fleet denying me area clearance to Vietnam. I still have that cable to this day.

It felt like fate intervened. Not long after, I learned that the Marine who had taken my place on that mission had been killed while on patrol.

I continued serving for nine months with the Third Reconnaissance Battalion as a platoon commander. Hoping to still contribute to the mission in Vietnam, I applied for a transfer to Division Headquarters in Okinawa, under G-2 (Intelligence). I believed that my French skills could still be put to use.

During this period, Henry Cabot Lodge continued his role advising the South Vietnamese government. One day, my commanding officer at G-2 pulled me aside and confided in me details about the assassination of South Vietnamese President Ngô Đình Diệm. I'll never forget his words: "Lieutenant, you cannot imagine how bloody our hands were in this matter." He explained how the CIA held the van's doors open for President Diệm and his brother while South Vietnamese Special Forces fired into the van, killing them both. The colonel believed that this act marked the beginning of the end for US involvement in Vietnam—severing the spiritual connection with the Vietnamese people, especially among the Buddhists who viewed Diệm as a godlike figure.

Still eager for more direct involvement, I had requested to remain with the Third Marine Division at the end of my tour. Instead, my next assignment came as a surprise—I was posted as a guard officer at the Brooklyn Navy Yard. The role was ceremonial in nature, involving sunset parades every Friday evening, much like those at the Marine Barracks at "8th and I" in Washington, D.C.

The colonel in charge insisted we maintain high standards, so dignitaries were invited to serve as reviewing officers. When top military brass weren't available, we brought in civilian figures—including, memorably, the president of Pepsi-Cola and Jenny Grossinger, a well-known hotelier. I'll never forget the sight of saluting that tiny woman while passing in review with my sword nearly sticking in the grass as I passed Jenny in a military salute.

Eventually, after nine months, I transferred to Camp Lejeune and served at the Infantry Training Regiment, where I was responsible for training troops in infantry tactics. I commanded a company training recruits, which was one of the rare episodes when Marines were recruited into what was historically an all-volunteer force. In my last three months, I finally had a chance to use my French as part of the interrogator-translator team with the Second Marine Division before resigning my commission.

When I told my commanding officer, Colonel Williams, that I was leaving the Corps, he tried to persuade me to stay. But I explained that my father—who had founded his business firm in Paris in 1929—was ready to pass it on to me. If I didn't return, he said he would liquidate the company. I couldn't bear to let that legacy disappear. And so, after four years of active duty, I resigned and returned to civilian life.

I didn't stay inactive for long. A Marine never really leaves emotionally. You are bound by history, tradition, camaraderie, and a warrior code to America's "911 Force." Twenty years later, I got a call from Tom Evans, a partner at Richard Nixon's law firm. He had read about my activist activities in the newspapers and asked if I'd be interested in becoming a trustee for the Marine Corps University Foundation. I accepted and eventually became president, then chairman.

My primary goal as chairman was to recruit a respected leader for the foundation—someone like General James Conway, former Commandant of the Marine Corps. After persistent effort, he agreed. I stepped down to vice-chairman so he could assume the top role, knowing that a four-star general brought the gravitas the foundation needed.

Today, I still have the letter from General Conway about my participation in his "kitchen cabinet," of which I was a member before he joined the Foundation, framed and hanging on my wall. Jim needed civilian former Marines to travel down to "The Tank," Washington, D.C., to advise him about events away from the nation's capital. Jim Conway was a picture-postcard Marine, having led his Marines in the bloody and victorious fight for Fallujah in Iraq.

5. ANGELS AND APRONS

My earliest memories are filled with narrow escapes and angelic luck—close brushes with danger that somehow always ended with me safe and sound. I like to believe there was an angel on my shoulder, watching over me.

One day, when I was around 2 years old—back when we were still living in Menthon-Saint-Bernard—I went out into the garden wearing the apron little French boys used to wear when they played outdoors. There, I found what I thought was a nest of worms. Delighted, I scooped them into my apron and hurried inside to show the family.

Suddenly, I was surrounded by screams—they weren't worms. They were vipers! My father knocked them out of my apron just in time, and one of the snakes turned on him, ready to strike. My brother, perhaps instinctively, stomped on its head. It could've just as easily been me who was bitten.

Another close call came shortly after. Behind our house, workers were sawing wood, and there was an exposed electric wire. To me, it looked like a great place to sit. As soon as I made contact, I was frozen—paralyzed by the high-voltage current. The workers quickly pulled me off and threw me into a cold bath to revive me. Somehow, once again, I survived.

But the most pivotal escape of all, of course, was escaping France as the war descended over Europe and that Swiss soldier who took out the Nazi about to end my five-year-old existence. That's a story I'll never forget. My first angel sighting.

My parents lived in Paris, and they were very much part of the café society that thrived before the war. They were regulars in the vibrant nightlife of that era—black-tie affairs, late nights, and the company of artists and thinkers. The Algonquin Group, Gertrude Stein, and F. Scott Fitzgerald—their world brushed shoulders with that same glamorous crowd. There's a portrait my father commissioned in 1932, painted by a man named Leon Lang. It still hangs in my family home.

My mother and I were very close. I was the middle child, and, by her own admission, I was her favorite. My older and younger brothers didn't always appreciate this—once, they even tried to smother me with a pillow. She caught them in the act and beat the hell out of them. She came from a wealthy Austrian family. After the collapse of the Austro-Hungarian Empire and her family's factory went bankrupt following World War I, she left Austria and ended up in a convent school. It didn't suit her. She eventually made her way to Paris, where she met my father—and it was love at first sight.

Their relationship had its challenges—the Catholic, Jewish juxtapositions for one—but they fell hard for each other and stayed fiercely united. They were like a Roman phalanx, shields locked—impossible to divide.

My father was a towering patriarchal figure. Tough, as you'd expect from someone who had survived both world wars. He cared deeply for his family, but he was strict, especially when it came to discipline. My mother stood right beside him in that, forming a solid front that no child could wedge apart.

When I was 10, everything changed. My mother fell very ill. In those days, there were no hormone treatments to help women through the emotional and physical upheaval that followed. She suffered terribly—mood swings, bouts of rage, and deep sorrow. I waited up for her on the top of the staircase steps of our house every evening, refusing to go to bed until she came home. To me, she was still like an angel, but one in pain.

Seeing her like that marked me. It left a deep impression. I developed a stutter. My thoughts raced, and I couldn't get the words out fast enough. It got so bad, my father turned to close friends for help—Tom Lovely and his wife Peggy, Irish friends from Jamaica Estates, and lovely they were. Their son, also Tom Jr., was an English professor at St. John's. Tom Senior had once been a Marine. Junior wasn't a speech therapist, but he understood how the mind worked. He came over, sat with me, and helped me slow my speech. "Your mind is going faster than your mouth," he told me. "You've got to balance the two." With his help, I overcame the stutter. But the emotional wound that caused it—that stayed with me.

My mother was beautiful, elegant, and self-conscious. I have photos of her in her youth that still take my breath away. One, in particular, shows her with my father on the steps of the villa in Menthon-Saint-Bernard. She endured so much, and I think that's why I've always had a soft spot for women in trouble. Maybe that's also why trouble has always had a soft spot for me. Either way, my angel endures.

6. STORMS, SECRETS, AND A WOMAN WITH A KNIFE

During my time with the US Marine Corps, I participated in joint operations with the South Korean Marines—the ROK Marines. We were stationed near K-3 Airfield in Kuryang-Po, near Pohang, South Korea, a location that had been used by the Allies during the Korean War.

When we first arrived, the battalion medical officer went into the village to check on the medical condition (venereal disease [VD]) of the prostitutes. His report was very bad. Much VD, and troops were advised to avoid the hookers, even though these Marines had been celibate for weeks on end. I gave my 30-man platoon a harsh warning in the morning and threatened them with "office hours" if they caught any diseases. In walking home that afternoon, a walking stick in hand, I suddenly heard a rustling sound in the nearby woods under the brush. As I approached, my entire platoon suddenly stood up, grabbing their trousers, with some tripping over them in their haste to clothe themselves.

The whole village entered the street from their homes to witness the spectacle of a young second lieutenant waving his walking stick as he chased a platoon of young marines out of the woods. The villagers laughed hysterically at this young teacher chasing after his pupils to instill some needed discipline. Beware the young man who hasn't seen a woman in months.

One day, a typhoon hit our tent encampment. As part of a reconnaissance battalion, we had a great deal of rolling stock—fast-moving vehicles like light armored tanks and personnel carriers designed to maneuver around the periphery of the division, scout enemy positions, and report back.

Lieutenant Colonel Nathan "Nat" Smith, our battalion commander, approached me in the middle of the storm. "Lieutenant," he said, "I understand you studied some geology at university?"

"Yes, sir," I replied.

"What do you think is happening?"

I looked at the skies clearing up and said, "Well, Colonel, I think we're in the eye of the typhoon. It's going to hit us again. The other side of the storm will get us!"

Taking my warning seriously, he moved the entire battalion, rolling stock and all, into a hangar for shelter. As fate would have it, the sun came out and stayed out. We had already been through the worst of it—the typhoon had passed. I'd misjudged it. For weeks after, and everywhere I was stationed in the Corps, there were whispers behind my back: "We're in the eye ..."

Still, better safe than sorry.

That reminds me of another adventure in 1963, during a deployment to the Philippines. Our battalion was assigned to conduct survival training in the jungles of Zambales. Each platoon, mine included—I was the platoon commander—was given one instruction: forage or starve. We were told outright, "No food will be provided. If you have to turn over rocks for snails, do it. Cook what you find and make do."

We weren't thrilled about the idea, but orders were orders. After a few days of scrounging and eating God-knows-what, morale was dipping fast. Then, out of the dense undergrowth, a small native man emerged—one of the Negritos, the indigenous people of the area. Tough as nails, these were the same tribes that had given the Japanese hell during World War II. Their resistance was legendary. I wouldn't be surprised if there were still a few skulls mounted on poles out there as a warning to intruders.

Without a word, the man gestured for us to follow. I hesitated for a beat, then rallied my band of exhausted Marines and trailed him into the jungle. We arrived in a small village tucked away in the brush, where he motioned for me to approach their chief.

The chief sat silently on a wooden throne, his foot swollen grotesquely from some sort of infection. The man who had led us there pointed at the foot, then turned to me and said in broken English, "You fix, Lieutenant?"

I blinked. "Oh, great," I muttered to myself. But I dug out my K-bar knife, sterilized it in flame, and pierced the swelling. Pus shot out, and the entire village stood in awe as I carried out impromptu field surgery under their watchful eyes.

It felt like a scene straight out of Indiana Jones and the Temple of Doom—one wrong move, and I figured I'd lose my head. But to my relief, the chief perked up almost immediately. By the next morning, he was up and about, walking without pain.

From that moment on, the tribe adopted us. They took in our whole platoon, fed us, looked after us. We came out of that village looking healthier than we had when we went in.

So much for survival training—we got five-star treatment in the middle of the Philippine jungle.

While I never saw combat during my military service, my life has had its fair share of dangerous moments—some of them far away from any battlefield.

One such incident happened years later in New York. It began innocently enough. I walked into an eyeglass store on Lexington Avenue called Ultimate Spectacle. That's where I met her. She was stunning—so beautiful, I did something I never usually do: I struck up a conversation with a complete stranger. She had conveniently left her personal information out on the counter. I called her later, and we started seeing each other.

She was Israeli, a sabra—tough, confident—but also a member of the Church of Scientology, something I didn't discover until it was too late. I've always considered that group a dangerous cult, and based on this experience, I stand by that belief.

What unfolded was surreal. I now believe our meeting was arranged by the church itself. Within days of meeting, she had me eating spiked marijuana brownies and, unbeknownst to me, spiking my mineral water with something far stronger—and so I would unknowingly succumb to the effects of the drugs. My daughter, Joelle, later confirmed it. She'd gone to drink from a bottle in the fridge when the woman yelled, "Don't touch that!" It was laced. That was for me. Joelle drank some and was heavily affected.

Under the influence, and swept up in whatever spell she had cast, I married her. Within two weeks, I realized the full horror of the situation. I hired a private investigator—his name was Serpico, a relative of the famous Frank Serpico—and he uncovered the truth: she was draining my bank accounts and was preparing to trap me further.

When she realized I was onto her, things took a violent turn. We were having a quiet glass of champagne in the apartment. I was trying to remain very calm. Suddenly, she shattered her glass and lunged at my throat. I knocked the shard out of her hand, but she ran to the kitchen and came back with a butcher knife—blade gleaming. I'll never forget it. The thing was at least eight inches long.

What saved me that day was instinct. I grabbed a chair and used it like a lion tamer to hold her off. She slashed over the top as I backed into the apartment's elevator corridor, pressed the elevator button, and prayed. The elevator doors opened—packed with people. She dropped the knife and calmly walked back inside as if nothing had happened.

But the damage was done. She had bitten my hand—hard enough that I had to be treated at the emergency room at Lenox Hill. Human bites can be incredibly dangerous, and this one broke skin.

I called the police immediately. They found her sitting serenely in the living room. I filed for divorce that day. She tried to take money, but in the end, I didn't owe her a dime. The entire ordeal took a year to legally untangle. She could have killed me.

The warning signs had been there. My parents were horrified when they heard about the wedding. Even my dear friend Clark Clifford, one of the most respected minds in Washington—who you will be reading a lot about—told me, "Don't do it." But I did it anyway.

It took time—real time—to legally unwind everything that had happened. When I filed for divorce, one crucial piece of the puzzle was finding the police officer who could testify that, when they arrived at the apartment, she was completely unharmed. I had never laid a finger on her. That detail was vital because, during the divorce proceedings, she attempted to paint a different picture.

I wracked my brain trying to remember the officer's name. And then it clicked: Angel Sosa. The name stuck with me because it reminded me of John Philip Sousa, the famous bandmaster of the United States Marine Corps. Sosa... Sousa—it rang a bell.

I went down to the police department and managed to track him down. Officer Angel Sosa agreed to testify in court. He was a wonderful man. Once he heard what had transpired—the drugs, the knife, the false claims—he said without hesitation, "Of course I'll testify."

Apparently, under the influence, she had convinced me to sign a document giving her half of my apartment. She tried to enforce that in court. But with Sosa's testimony, the judge saw through the ruse and threw it out. "Absolutely not," the court ruled. She walked away with nothing. She then had to flee the country as Serpico uncovered where she had hidden a lot of valuable antiques taken from my apartment. Bon débarras!—Good riddance!

The entire episode, from the moment I married her to the time I filed for divorce, spanned just a few chaotic weeks. We'd known each other a bit longer—we'd even traveled together. I visited her in Israel. Her family adored me. Her brother, in particular, was a genuinely kind man. But she… she was twisted in ways I couldn't have imagined.

Even now, I'm convinced the Church of Scientology orchestrated our meeting. That encounter in the eyeglass shop was no coincidence. She worked at a different branch of Ultimate Spectacle—several blocks away. She had no reason to be in that particular store, at that particular time, pretending to be shopping. And yet, there she was, perfectly placed. But I had a scheduled appointment at the store. I was targeted—by her, or perhaps by someone else in the Church of Scientology—who had, no doubt, read about me in the newspapers.

What began as a charming flirtation became a brush with death. What followed was a courtroom drama with high stakes. And what lingered afterward was a deepened instinct for caution—and the lasting comfort that, somehow, I had once again been protected. Maybe by luck. Maybe by instinct. Or maybe, just maybe, that angel on my shoulder was still doing his job. But cutting my own path has always come at a price.

7. FROM A USMC INFANTRY OFFICER TO GLOBAL FINANCE

WITH AN MBA ON THE WAY

After my tour in the Far East, my next nine months in the Marine Corps were spent at the Brooklyn Navy Yard, serving as a guard officer—a ceremonial post, but one that came with an unexpected benefit. It allowed me to take night classes at New York University's Graduate School of Business. The campus was conveniently located downtown, just across from my father's office at 50 Broadway. In that time, I completed all the core requirements toward a master's degree. It's even noted on my discharge papers: core coursework completed at New York University.

As I was preparing to leave the Corps, my father asked me the inevitable question:

"So, hotshot, what are you going to do now that you're a civilian?"

I told him, "I'm going to get an MBA."

He looked at me blankly. "What's that?"

That was my father—an old-school European gentleman through and through. I explained, "Dad, in the United States, if you want to get anywhere in business, you need an MBA. You need the sheepskin." He nodded, then said something that would shape the next phase of my life:

"Fine. You go to school at night—and you work for me during the day."

Two days after my discharge in June 1966, I started working for my father. No break. No transition. Just straight in.

There is, admittedly, one personal detour in that timeline. As I was making my way up from Camp Lejeune, I stopped at the Officers Club in Virginia

Beach and met a woman. We hit it off. When I returned to New York, she followed—and called me. She was a knockout. My father saw right through it.

"No," he said, flatly. "You start work tomorrow."

Well, that was that. When I think about that lady, I recall she was rather fetching, but I was honor-bound not to take it further for one very simple reason: her husband was a Marine fighter pilot in Vietnam. But that's how my career began: grounded, focused, and very much under the watchful eye of my father.

The first six months on the job, I worked from home. My parents had moved to a grand, antique-filled apartment in Chatsworth Gardens in Larchmont, New York. It had high ceilings, floor-to-ceiling windows, and the unmistakable air of European sophistication.

About three months in, I was preparing for a business training trip to Europe while my parents had left on vacation. One morning, rushing to get into Manhattan, I forgot to close those massive windows. A windstorm blew through Larchmont, knocking over priceless furniture and artwork, resulting in many broken antiques on the apartment floor. I called my father in a panic.

"You've got to warn Mom," I said.

She returned home, took one look at the wreckage, then at my bandaged head—I'd just been in a car accident a few days earlier, smashing my forehead into the windshield in my Volkswagen on the Hutchinson River Parkway—and she declared:

"I know exactly what happened. You had an orgy in this apartment."

There was no convincing her otherwise. Not then. Not ever.

Soon after, I was sent to Europe to meet my father's clients and gain international experience. I spent three months in Amsterdam working for a private bank—some of his closest connections. They were a truly lovely family: Peter and Joké Meyer Swantee and their two children, Hans and Christine. Peter was head of Kol&Co. bankers. Then I moved to Brussels, where I trained with a a close family associate, friend, and colleague named Jean Peterbroeck, the head of Peterbroeck Van Kempenhout & Co., the leading brokerage firm in Belgium.

Jean would later become godfather to my son Jamie, after losing his own son in a tragic skiing accident. It was a gesture that cemented our deep and profound friendship and our business relationship.

Before I arrived in Belgium, my father had called Jean and said, "Find him a quiet place to stay. Somewhere safe."

He did. I was placed in a charming pension—essentially a bed and breakfast—run by an elderly woman named Madame Honoré. Fittingly, she lived on Rue de Balzac. Madame Honoré on Rue de Balzac—it doesn't get more French than that.

The staff at the bank were surprised and impressed by my American willingness to challenge convention. So much so that the bank's chairman, Maurice Naessens, personally praised my father and then sent me on to Paris to meet a rather infamous figure: Serge Varangot, the public face of Paribas stock operations. I walked into his office, shook his hand, and he handed me his "Carte de Visite"—which I still have. He looked at me squarely in the eyes and said:

> "Yes, I have heard of your father. But I know Salem Lewis, head of risk arbitrage at Bear Stearns. Your father does not figure amongst the top people in that field."

The Pig!

I contained my rage long enough to crush his limp hand with a Marine's grip, about-faced, and marched out. If only Serge had known the truth. My father was a mathematical genius, able to calculate numbers with supernatural ease. During his university days in Hungary, a family friend named Peter Green sent an agent to find the most brilliant student in the country. They found my father.

Peter Green's firm—Pichler & Co., a respected banking firm in Vienna—immediately hired him, and quickly dazzled the partners. So much so, they sent him to their Paris office to run arbitrage operations—and that's where his legend began.

At the time, blocked currency restrictions made it impossible to buy certain securities in places like Budapest and Vienna, even though those same securities traded freely in Paris—often at significantly higher prices. The spread was an arbitrageur's dream, if only one could get around the currency regulations. My father could.

He created a dummy cable company and began sending coded telegrams—purportedly for legitimate cable messages—to secretly move money across borders. With local currency in hand, he'd buy discounted shares, ship them to Paris, and sell them to the willing "quacking ducks" of the market. He made Pichler & Co. a fortune.

Naturally, he struck out on his own. In the fateful year of 1929, no less. Somehow, he survived the crash and found new footing as a floor broker on the Bourse de Paris. That lasted until the outbreak of war in 1940. After that, he didn't work again until we returned to France in 1945.

In 1939, my father inadvertently caused quite a commotion on the Paris Bourse. Tensions were already high across France, as Hitler's aggression in Poland had everyone on edge. My father, needing to execute a trade, called out for his floor broker—whose name, quite fittingly, was LaGuerre.

"Laguerre! Laguerre!" he shouted across the trading floor.

But in a charged atmosphere where every whisper of conflict could ignite panic, his call was misheard—or perhaps simply misinterpreted. Traders froze, then erupted into chaos, convinced he was announcing that war—la guerre—had officially begun with Germany.

Pandemonium swept the exchange floor. Of course, the actual outbreak of war came later—on May 10, 1940—when Hitler sent Heinz Guderian's XIX SS Panzer Corps crashing through the Ardennes and into France. Uncle Tony, as fate would have it, was with that very attacking force.

But survival was never in doubt. He had protected the family with foresight and genius. First, by buying a chicken farm, and then hiring a cook who could prepare fifty different kinds of noodles. We had noodles for breakfast, noodles for dinner, and sugared noodles for dessert. We never went hungry.

That was my father: a man who could outsmart borders, banks, and bureaucrats—and still ensure his family was fed when the world collapsed.

But back to Brussels. Alas, at this point I had become restless, in addition to being harassed by the woman's aggressive daughter, who would chase me around the dining table, halitosis, and all. So, weekends couldn't come fast enough. I bought a brand-new Karmann Ghia from the Volkswagen factory in Wolfsburg, Germany—a sleek, convertible sports car. Every weekend, I raced through the Belgian countryside, top down, en route to Paris. It was a 5-hour drive, passing through Mons and past the SHAPE headquarters.

Once, I stopped for gas in a small town, and a group of schoolchildren gathered around the car. One little boy exclaimed,

"Quelle jolie petite voiture!"

("What a beautiful little car!")

It was a sweet moment I never forgot.

Six months later, I was ready to extend my European training. But my father summoned me back.

"We're merging with Bache & Company," he said.

It was July of 1967. The reason? More capital. The merger gave us significant financial strength—but it also revealed some of my father's doubts. He wasn't sure I could handle the technicalities or the pressure. He even considered bringing in my younger brother, Chris, who worked in investment banking at A.G. Becker in Chicago. But Chris didn't want any part of it—he and my father clashed. I, the middle child, was the diplomat. I could get along.

Still, tensions grew. One day, fed up with my father's overbearing management, I left his division and joined the corporate finance department at Bache. It was a shock to him—a loss of face. But eventually, his elders lured me back with a promotion, a raise, and a new title: his assistant.

When my father retired in 1971, the question arose: Would I be given the leadership role?

That's when Clark Clifford stepped in.

A powerful and respected man, he wrote to John Leslie and followed up with a call.

"This young man," he said, "has been handling my account. He knows exactly what he's doing. I've read his MBA thesis. You have to give him a shot."

They listened. And the rest, as they say, is history.

Clark was more than a mentor—he was a guardian and a surrogate father. He once told me, "If I ever had a son, he'd have been just like you."

He had four daughters. I imagine that came with its own kind of trouble. But I never forgot those words.

8. RISK ARBITRAGE—WHAT IT IS AND WHY I OPENED IT UP TO WALL ST

This is an excerpt from my book, *Risk Arbitrage*, to save you from reading the whole book. Unless you're a finance enthusiast—or just enjoy pain.

The simple definition of "arbitrage"—buying an article in one market and selling it in another—has undergone considerable refinement over the decades. Arbitrage had its origin in the late medieval period when Venetian merchants traded interchangeable currencies in order to profit from price differentials. This "classic" arbitrage, as it was and continues to be carried on, is a practically riskless venture in that the profit, or spread, is assured by the convertibility of the instruments involved.

Communications, rudimentary as they were, assumed strategic importance on the European financial scene. The notable London merchant bank of Rothschild, as the story goes, staged an unprecedented "coup de bourse" by use of carrier pigeons to receive advance notice of Wellington's victory at Waterloo. Upon learning the news, Rothschild began, with much ado, selling various securities, particularly British government bonds, on the London Stock Exchange. This was naturally interpreted as a Wellington defeat, thereby precipitating a panicky selling wave. The astute—and informed—Rothschild then began quietly purchasing, through stooges, all the government bonds that were for sale. When an earthbound messenger finally brought the news of an allied victory, Rothschild had a handsome profit.

As identical securities began to be traded on the different European exchanges, and as communications evolved from the pigeon to the wireless, simultaneous transactions in securities arbitrage gave way to "tendency" arbitrage. Thus, if, for example, one had good wire communications with London and Paris, where an identical security was being traded, one would try to detect a general market tendency in both markets. Should there prove to be sellers in London and buyers in Paris, an arbitrageur would sell into the buying in Paris, and try to cover his short position somewhat later when the selling tendency bottomed out in London, or vice versa. In any event, improved market liquidity and more advanced communications were providing the opportunity for "tendency" as well as "simultaneous" transactions.[1]

Riskless arbitrage found its way into the American securities market by way of instruments that are convertible into common stock (i.e., convertible bonds and convertible preferred stocks, rights, and warrants). This kind of arbitrage, according to Morgan Evans, "… is not a wild scramble of buying X common in New York, then selling it in San Francisco in a matter of moments, like the international arbitrageur who buys Shell Trading in Amsterdam and sells it in New York. Instead, it is chiefly concerned with the buying of a security at one price and the selling of its equivalent (security) at a higher price, usually in the same market. Convertibility of exchangeability lies solely in one direction. In this respect it differs from two-way convertibility or exchangeability, which is associated with the foreign exchange markets."

There were two distinct developments in the 1930s that had a profound influence on the evolution of arbitrage in the United States. First, many railroads in the late 1930s were coming out of bankruptcy. In order to remove their heavy debt burdens and improve their capital structures, many of them were reorganized (i.e., recapitalized). These reorganization plans, which had to be approved by the various classes of security holders, often required the issuance of new securities to be exchanged for the old debt and preferred issues. Arbitrageurs, finding that they could sell such new securities on a "when-issued" basis, would buy the shares being recapitalized at prices lower than, or below the parity of, these "when-issued" securities. These price discrepancies, or spreads, were available because of the inherent risk that the reorganization plan might not be consummated, thereby precluding the requisite one-way convertibility. The arbitrageur was able to take advantage of the spread and was willing to incur the risk. Arbitrage was now moving, in fact, from riskless to risk operations.

The second and equally important development in this period was the 1935 Public Utility Holding Company Act, requiring many public utilities to divest themselves of their holdings of subsidiaries. As the parent companies formulated divestiture plans, "when-issued" markets developed not only in the shares of their subsidiaries, but also in the stock of the parent ex-distributions. Arbitrage was thus possible when the sum of the prices of these "when-issued" securities (i.e., the sum of the parts) was greater than the market price of the parent company (the whole) cum distributions.

"The profits realized from these recapitalizations and reorganizations led the arbitrageur ultimately to exploit the stock price differentials, or spreads, available in mergers, liquidations, and tender offers."[3] The spreads were, however, only turned into profit when the necessary one-way convertibility of the riskless arbitrage became a legal fact through consummation.

The expansion of risk arbitrage on Wall Street is directly attributable to the great corporate merger wave of the 1960s, when a surging supply of selling candidates was matched by an equally impressive list of buyers. The new notion of "synergy," that one plus one equals three, gained acceptability; inflated stock prices provided cheap financing in an ever-tightening money market; accounting for acquisitions on a "pooling of interests" basis permitted seductive pro forma earnings calculations for acquisition-minded companies; and most important, a variety of tax savings was intensively exploited via a variety of security-exchange packages.

While this 1960s merger wave enabled the arbitrageur to develop expertise in the realm of risk arbitrage, the trade itself continued to generate new types of situations where the professional could apply a sharp pencil. In addition to mergers and recapitalizations, then, risk arbitrage came to encompass stock tender offers, cash tender bids, stub situations, and spinoffs. As the number of synergistic mergers declines in weak securities and tight monetary markets, liquidity or necessitous mergers and un-merging activities are providing work for the enlarged arbitrage community.

THE ARBITRAGE COMMUNITY

"The big money makers of Wall Street often mask their expertise in mystery, and among them, the most mysterious is a cliquish band of specialists known as arbitrageurs. On the Street, they are a peculiar group apart, noted for their ability to spot instantly tiny profits that can be jockeyed into big ones. 'It would take me an hour of paperwork to see that profit,' says one member of the New York Stock Exchange, 'and in that hour the chance would be gone.' Says another: 'I think of them as vague shadows with European backgrounds. I don't even know who they are.'"[4] Arbitrageurs love it that way.

The financial press has increasingly tried to explore the activities of the risk arbitrageurs over the past few years, yet has been unable to delve with any depth into their operations. Many arbitrageurs have been approached, but have been generally unhelpful, though congenial. "Arbitrageurs tend to keep their operations to themselves. 'Frankly, I'd prefer the average person didn't know how to accomplish arbitrage,' says one. 'Therefore, the less I say about it, the better.'" Even Morgan Evans, whose *Arbitrage in Domestic Securities in the United*

States surpasses anything yet published on the subjects of both riskless and risk arbitrage, falls short in explaining the modus operandi of these professionals.

The arbitrage community, then, consists of a dozen-plus Wall Street firms that commit house capital as one of their primary functions, in the various forms of arbitrage. The list includes such outstanding firms as Lehman Brothers-Kuhn Loeb, Goldman Sachs, L.F. Rothschild, Morgan Stanley, and Salomon Brothers.

Many of the arbitrage firms will engage the capital of foreign banks in risk arbitrage situations. Most are reluctant to do so for domestic clients, as the latter are thought to be somewhat less discreet than their European counterparts. Some, in order to avoid conflicts of interest, will avoid arbitrage for client accounts altogether.

The community is extremely cliquish. Each member of the club has his own particular set of friends within the community with whom he will freely exchange ideas and information, often via direct private wires. Sometimes good friends will even work on a joint account for a particular deal. But to all others, both within and without the community, the member will turn a cold shoulder. Many Wall Street firms and many private investors have tried, at one time or another, to participate in risk arbitrage activity. Having neither (a) schooling or experience in the finer points of the trade, (b) the requisite expert staff, nor (c) membership in the community, they tend to fall by the wayside.

The cancellation of a few proposed mergers always singles out the amateurs and sends them scurrying back to the good old-fashioned business of investing in securities. Any proper discussion of the Wall Street arbitrage community's changing dynamics over recent decades would be incomplete without some consideration of the context in which these professional traders were operating. For it has always been the talent of the skilled arbitrageur to distill from a complex and ever-changing marketplace, those opportunities that others fail to capture. As the most popular, or, as some might say, "notorious" community of arbs operated primarily in the field of mergers and acquisitions, a brief synopsis of the developments of the structure of the M&A business is essential for any student in assessing the challenges that confronted arbs as they adapted and thrived in the growing world of risk arbitrage. The mergers and acquisitions business as it existed in the late 1960s may seem like a foreign landscape to today's student of Wall Street practices. While each passing decade has brought new developments in the structure and pace of the deal market, the 1970s and 1980s were particularly formative years in laying the groundwork for the modern deal structure. Indeed, few developments in recent years match the pace of innovation seen during this critical period. The arbitrageur who ventured into these markets needed to be both agile and somewhat innovative in his own right. With the public face of the arbitrageurs, as well as the banker, and other participants, in the deal community becoming clearer, their activities gained notoriety not seen before on Wall Street. The takeover battles of the 1970s assumed a "spectator sport" appeal to the rest of the financial and business community. Amid the growing deal frenzy, arbitrageurs grappled with an ever-changing terrain, formed by the ebb and flow of the economic, political, financial, and legislative conditions that were all refocused during this profound reshaping of corporate America.

9. BACHE & COMPANY

I completed my MBA in 1971, and I joined my dad's firm in June 1966; then, in 1967, he decided to merge his company with Bache & Company, a large retail brokerage firm. Bache eventually became Prudential-Bache, which is still in existence today. My dad stayed around for a few months after relinquishing his position to me, making sure I could handle the job—a lot of people thought I couldn't. But I took to it pretty naturally. He taught me halfway to death, and a lot of what's in my first book, *Risk Arbitrage*, was a roadmap of his mind.

I remember the first arbitrage deal I did. Dad gave me a range of three or four deals, and I put some money in, but the first one didn't go through. Then, the second one didn't go through, and I was starting to get discouraged. Then a third one didn't go through, and he started getting really nervous, but—thank God—I closed the fourth one, and it more than made up for the other three—I was off to the races and never looked back.

In 1971, I took over the Bache & Company Arbitrage Department, but it didn't happen easily. In fact, this is an important part of my life story. One of my closest friends was Clark Clifford. Clark had been the Secretary of Defense under Lyndon Johnson. He was a White House adviser to Harry Truman, JFK, Jimmy Carter, and even Gerald Ford, at times, would pull him in. Clark was the one whom Lyndon Johnson commissioned to go and find out the truth about the domino theory in the Pacific. The "domino theory," a Cold War concept, posited that if one country fell to communism, neighboring nations would also succumb, leading to a domino effect of communist expansion, particularly in Southeast Asia. As Clark related to me when he left the Defense Department, he said, "I had kept hearing about the domino theory, so I went and talked to the dominoes. The dominoes didn't care. That's when I convinced LBJ to stop the bombing of North Vietnam." He had worked for Admiral Forrestall before he joined Truman, so he had a remarkable depth of experience. So much so that he admonished Kennedy over the Bay of Pigs—he said to him, "Jack, you can never do this again. This was a big mistake. You can't train somebody, throw them in the middle of the battlefield like that, and then desert them. We had aircraft support and a carrier offshore. We could have wiped Castro out right then and there, but you didn't have the nerve. Never do this again."

Evidently, Clark was no shrinking violet, and he was like a surrogate father to me. I couldn't have had a better guy to sit there on my wing, advising me. He had me manage all his money, and he had a lot of it—being a successful lawyer from St. Louis and then joining the ranks of the Democratic advisors over the years. He had to sell everything when he joined the Defense Department and had huge capital losses on his shares, so I said, "I can use those capital losses and make it up with short-term gains for you, investing in arbitrage transactions." My strategy made it all back for him, which positioned me well for what was about to happen.

I first got involved with Clark when I was using his law firm in Washington. His firm was called Clifford & Miller. He was the senior partner, and I was using his antitrust specialist because a lot of what we do in the arbitrage strategy gets tangled up with antitrust matters. Two companies merging raise a lot of red flags, as you can imagine. One day, Clark asked his chief of the antitrust investigation section, whose name was Larry Williams, "Who is this guy who's using us for antitrust advice?" Williams replied, "Oh, I'm in touch with him every day on these matters—he's written a thesis." Clark raises an eyebrow and says, "Really? Let me read it." So, Clark reads the thesis, calls me up, and he says, "Come down and have lunch with me." I, of course, took the next plane, sat in his office, and was completely enthralled. What a charming guy this guy was. Just one of those truly remarkable men. His wife used to tell me that he was like catching a comet by the tail. Anyhow, after the meeting, I went back to New York. Two days later, I got a check in the mail for a million bucks. I invested it, and to make a long story short, we wound up managing 20–30 million dollars of his money, and we used up all the capital losses he had. In addition, he didn't pay a dime of tax when making it back, so he was forever grateful to me for that.

Unfortunately, he got into some trouble at the end of his life with Averell Harriman's wife, Pamela. Clark had decided that—when in 1987 a severe market crash struck—he didn't want to be in stocks anymore, so he got cajoled into investing with a guy named Brennan, a crook doing real estate deals in New Jersey. He lost a lot of money for the Harriman family. He was already retired, but as a point of honor, he wanted to pay her back for everything he'd lost the family. And he did. He signed the agreement to pay them off, and the next day, he passed away.

I always think of that, you know. It was just an amazing story of courage. He was not very well; he'd had open heart surgery, but this was a guy who would call me from an operating table and say, "Well, how did you get yourself into this mess?" Particularly with women. And he'd say things like, "What's the matter with you? I told you, if you see something you can't do without, at least be discreet."

In the early 1980s, he decided to diversify his interests and was asked to become the chairman of Financial General Bancshares. The bank was so thrilled to have Clark in that role that they gave him his office in the D.C. branch. Clark had to convince bank regulators that there was no foreign influence in the bank's ownership. He prevailed, until the day it was learned that four Arab sheiks, associated with the Pakistani group BCCI, had a controlling share in the bank transferred unforeseen into their control through BCCI's Luxembourg branch. This became the huge BCCI scandal in 1990 and almost took my friend Clark down. The *Wall Street Journal* was particularly vicious about his participation in the bank's management. This was, after all, the dean, the elder statesman of the Democrats. Clark, under great pressure, suffered a heart attack, requiring open heart surgery. It was incumbent on me to do something to help Clark, who had so often helped me. I wrote to the presiding judge a letter in support of Clark that I do believe is a must read. I think it helped. Clark was acquitted.

When he recovered, Clark decided to reenter society in D.C. by having me join him for lunch at the prestigious Metropolitan Club. All his friends from the D.C. establishment were there. They were so happy to find Clark had recovered. I was so impressed to see the warmth they bestowed upon him, particularly by the famous CNN anchor team of Evans & Novak.

Clark Clifford was the principal reason I got to take over my father's position. When all the doubters came around, Clark Clifford told them, "You give this guy his chance; he can do it." If Clark didn't have all that experience with me managing his money, and if he and I hadn't been like father and son, I wouldn't have had anyone to back me. Everyone has a story about being pulled over the hump, and if ever somebody pulled me over the hump, it was Clark Clifford. I supposed I'd made some enemies. Nothing serious, but occasionally, I'd rub people the wrong way if I went after one of their companies. I once went after McGraw-Hill, for instance. It was McGraw's annual meeting, and I went to the mat with the management because they had gotten an offer from American Express that they wouldn't even consider. Everyone has their agenda, but from a shareholder's perspective, this was good business, so I went in hard.

This is the letter I wrote to Judge Bradley advocating for Clark Clifford. An important example of how I approach activism. With passion and a sense of purposeful justice.

December 1, 1992
The Honorable John A.K. Bradley
Justice of the Supreme Court of New York
111 Centre Street
Room 1133
New York, NY 10013

Dear Judge Bradley:

I am writing you at a moment when you are about to make a grave decision regarding the future of one of America's most respected elder statesmen. You will decide whether Clark Clifford must stand trial for an alleged role in the BCCI affair.

I observe with increasing indignation and outrage the vilification and inhumane treatment being dealt to one of the great men of the twentieth century, Clark McAdams Clifford. Is there none amongst us who would speak for this man? The silence is deafening, yet the days pass by as this magnificent man is left slowly twisting in the wind. For what is at stake is his very life. The doctors say that if the threat of undergoing a trial is not removed, this 86 year old will undoubtedly not survive. He no longer has the luxury which our system affords: to prove his innocence.

Yet there must be those who know him well who would speak in his behalf and so counter the usual prosecutorial leaks and the public lynching for which the Fourth Estate so eagerly clamors. Is it too cynical to think that the recently concluded electoral contest prevents his numerous Democratic Party colleagues from speaking out? Or likewise the world's leaders who have known him, but hobbled by their own domestic problems, avoid the messy implications of the BCCI affair by hiding behind the safety of their stony silence? Would it not rather do honor to these men to make themselves now heard?

Your Honor, I believe justice requires a simple glance at Clark Clifford's contributions to his country—and to the Free World—in order to assess the allegations of his detractors.

I cannot believe that this person's manifest love of country and dedicated public service to four American presidents would permit him to betray all that for which he stands! His accomplishments? A few of the more salient in which his guiding hand was instrumental:

The Truman Doctrine
The Marshall Plan
The creation of the National Security Council and the CIA
The reorganization of the Armed Forces under the Joint Chiefs of Staff
The recognition of the State of Israel
The ceasing of the bombing of North Vietnam and the reversal of America's involvement in Vietnam

One can perceive in the above the very cornerstone of America's Post World War II security, the containment of Soviet communism and its eventual undoing. Would Clark Clifford then forsake these critical accomplishments by allegedly putting an important American banking institution at risk? I think not.

Clark Clifford is charged with allegedly assisting foreign interests in illegally gaining control of Financial General Bancshares. The gravamen of the case against him centers on whether or not he knew that these seemingly respectable Arab investors were, in effect, nominees for BCCI. The Bank of England didn't know, neither did our own Federal Reserve Board, or BCCI's own accountants, Price Waterhouse. How could they? How could Clifford? The illicit transfer of shares was carried out by the "bank within a bank", shrouded in the secrecy afforded by a tax haven, the Grand Duchy of Luxembourg.

Personally, I know in my heart that Clark Clifford didn't know. I handled the bulk of his investments for 15 years. We discussed many things in that time. As absurd as this now appears with the benefit of hindsight, I know that he believed that Mr. Abedi was a visionary who would provide loans for poor Moslems around the world. I knew Clark Clifford's investment profile well. When it came to the Bank over which he presided he wanted to invest in it because he felt confident that he and his team would make it prosper and that it would double and triple in value over time. He saw it as "a unique opportunity." I believed him then as I believe him now.

Your Honor, I entreat you to save this man for should some harm befall him, it would be a blot on our National conscience that we had dealt so unfairly with one who has in so many ways protected us and the very freedoms we cherish.

Yours Respectfully,

Guy P. Wyser-Pratte
President
Wyser-Pratte

10. THE ARC OF THE ARBITRAGE INDUSTRY

A CHANGING COMMUNITY FROM THE 1970S TO 2000

The 1970s saw the initial deal wave of the late sixties gather considerable momentum and, in the process, broaden the variety and the style of acquisition structure available to the corporate buyer. With mixed reactions from within the community, it also introduced the arbitrageur to the public. As could be expected, attention begets even greater attention, and by the end of the decade, the arbitrageur might be said to be swimming in a sea of deals—and arbitrageurs! The 1970s could best be characterized as the years that propelled the M&A business toward increasingly novel and flexible deal structures. The unfolding techniques were more aggressive, the press more inquisitive, and the once congenial club of arbitrageurs who plied their expertise out of only a handful of firms found themselves in a market crowded by newer players.

One of the more significant developments, foreshadowed by the 1969 hostile takeover bid for BF Goodrich by Northwest Industries, was the first truly large-scale hostile cash tender offer. Launched in 1974 by Inco for ESB Corporation, the offer was significant not only for this new currency of the hostile offer, but also for what it represented: a bold new dimension in the world of deal-making. The significance to the arb community was in the additional arrow it placed in the quiver of the would-be corporate buyer and, of course, the modification of the risk/reward considerations for those who assumed positions in such deals. Any expansion in the options available to bidder corporations expands in equal measure the profitable opportunities for the arbitrageur. In taking an offer directly to the shareholders, the debate over the appropriate balance between a board's fiduciary obligations and shareholders' rights began inching toward center stage—a position it would firmly occupy decades later. As "shareholder-friendly" generally equated to "arb-friendly," the new hostile tenders were, of course, greeted with open arms.

The decade was not finished with innovation, however, and the next change to come would involve the allocation of the payment that the arbitrageur received. Typically, a tender offer for control is followed by a squeeze-out merger to bring the bidder to 100% control. Conventional expectations at this time were that an owner of stock acquired in a deal, whether hostile or friendly, would receive equal monetary consideration on both the front and back ends. The value of cash or non-cash consideration paid in the first-stage tender offer would equal the consideration on the back end. The first significant departure from this assumption took place in the takeover fight for Pullman between McDermott and Wheelabrator Frye. McDermott offered a package that featured cash on the front end, with back-end securities that were markedly lower in value than the front. Ultimately, Pullman was acquired by Wheelabrator in a white knight rescue, but the "two-tiered" offer had arrived. It altered some of the financial constraints normally associated with the structure and financing of a bid, adding to the deal frenzy by allowing for more creatively structured deals and a reduced reliance on cash in a hostile approach.

The arbitrage community, while enjoying the increase in deal volume, was less excited by the new entrants it attracted to the business. The arb's return on investment is a direct function of the demand for that particular spread. With five or six arbs willing to trade a deal for no less than a 25% annualized return, the arrival of a new player who is willing to accept 20% compresses the profit available to the others. The new player will bid up the target's price while selling down the acquirer's price, leaving those who require a higher return outside or "away" from the market. This new crowding of the arb market can best be described in the words of the arbs themselves during this period, as printed in a story run by Barron's.

By the seventies ... the arbitrage community was having difficulty hiding its role in the mounting volume of corporate takeovers. In 1975, Ivan Boesky, lawyer, accountant, and securities analyst, established what probably was the first large limited partnership specializing in risk arbitrage. Boesky, to attract capital and much to the disgust of the rest of the community, stomped all over the unwritten rule proscribing publicity. "Boesky was the first of the queens to come out of the closet," says Alan Slifka, a partner in L.F. Rothschild Unterberg Towbin's arbitrage division. In 1977, Boesky was spread across two pages of Fortune, wreathed in smiles over the $30 million he and a handful of other arbitrageurs had picked up in the takeover of Babcock & Wilcox by United Technologies. The jig was up!

Money poured into risk arbitrage. Merrill Lynch and Morgan Stanley quickly set up arbitrage departments. Many experienced arbitrageurs formed their own limited partnerships, and a whole slate of smaller firms joined the act.

With quality firms selling for bargain-basement multiples, it had become cheaper for a company to acquire another than to make a capital investment itself. But the flat equity markets also meant that takeover stocks became "the only game in town"—a game in which hungry registered representatives were eager to interest equity-shy clients. At least two large brokerages, Oppenheimer & Co. and Bear Stearns, launched an organized assault, publishing research for retail and institutional clients. No figures are available, but the guesstimate is that as much as half the arbitrage activity in some deals was "non-professional."

"A shakeout is the best thing that could happen in this business," says John Monk, an arbitrageur at Cohn, Delaire and Kaufman. Chief among Monk's beefs is the narrowed spreads brought about by too many players jockeying for a piece of the same action. "The single greatest complaint I hear these days is the spreads," Monk says. "A few years ago, if $25 was bid for a company, you might see it open up at $19 or $20. Everybody was reasonable. Today, spreads are nothing."

Disorderly markets are another problem. "There are 33,000 registered reps out there," continues Monk, "and they can cause severe dislocation in the market. The non-professionals tend to get out at the first sign of trouble, dumping all their stock back into the market."

Complains Steve Hahn of Easton & Co., "There never used to be any problem of getting as much stock as you wanted. Now I find sometimes I'll go after 5,000 shares of something and only be able to get, say, 3,000." But arbitrageurs used to dealing in blocks ten or a hundred times larger scoff at such squawks. Their sanguine philosophy is that "when the going gets tough, the tough get going." Says one whose firm is believed to put some $100 million at the disposal of its arbitrage department: "Markets have a magnificent way of correcting themselves. For example, if you take a situation like we saw with Marathon, where the stock was quickly run up to $90 after the Mobil bid of $85, you'll find that most of that was non-professional or inexperienced money. Not till the stock came down again to the low eighties did you find the arb money coming in a significant way."

Certainly, the year was trying for professionals and non-professionals alike. Stratospheric interest rates dampened most investment sectors. High rates cut two ways in arbitrage. On the one hand, the carrying costs must be factored into the spreads on any given deal, although one arbitrageur declares: "If the difference between 15 percent and 20 percent interest rates is the deciding factor in whether you do a deal, you probably shouldn't be even considering it in the first place."

It is the author's contention that the private as well as the institutional investor should be more conversant with risk arbitrage, for it often appears as though one-half of the list on the New York Stock Exchange would like to swallow the other half. Thus, stocks involved in mergers and other forms of risk arbitrage will often perform in accordance with other than their fundamental or technical characteristics. In addition, the average investor should know how to evaluate a particular package of securities offered in exchange for those securities that he is holding. The answers to some of these problems will enable the investor to make an important investment decision: whether to hold his position in the security, or dispose of it. It is thus the author's intention to explain and describe these market reactions by discussing the various activities in which the arbitrageur gets involved.

Whereas in the first edition of *Risk Arbitrage* there was extensive coverage of merger arbitrage reflecting the emphasis of the 1960s, cash tender offers became much more important in the 1970s and 1980s and are given greater coverage in later sections. Indeed, cash tenders became the favorite vehicle for effecting what were called "Saturday Night Specials," or hostile tender offers. It will be shown in the examples that follow that participation in these cash tender offers was far more profitable for the arbitrage community than participation in mergers, in that the former usually forced the target brides to seek competitive bids.

1980s

The 1980s brought the arbitrage business to new heights on the back of the largest takeover boom to date. Propelling the expansion in deals was the introduction of high-yield bonds, or "junk" financing, for hostile takeovers. The concept of purchasing a corporation using its own assets as the collateral had been long pondered but not put to significant use with public companies. This decade brought such action and did so on a scale never before imagined. The prowess of Michael Milken's junk bond desk at Drexel Burnham Lambert was such that, at times, it seemed that no deal was too big or too bold to be launched. The unbridled success, or some may say, excess of Drexel financing and those who profited from it would ultimately end in the indictment of arbitrageur Ivan Boesky, and later Milken, in a widespread insider trading scandal. Alongside these developments came the beginnings of the collapse of the junk bond market and Drexel itself. But not before this financing machine and the man who ran it left an indelible mark on both M&A and the arbitrage business.

What Milken created was a market for corporate raider debt obligations. Milken's new debt instruments stood on their own, requiring no convertibility to equity. They allowed the corporate raider to, among other things, finance a bid entirely in cash and work around the Mill's Bill, which had disallowed the deduction of interest on takeover debt linked to equity. A raider needed only a "highly confident" letter from Drexel that it could raise the necessary financing, and it could be assured that its intentions would be taken seriously by the Street and a target's board.

The 1980s also brought an increase in the frequency of "white knight" rescues. Among some notable examples were DuPont's 1981 winning bid for Conoco following an initial bid from Seagrams and Occidental Petroleum's 1982 rescue of Cities Service from T. Boone Pickens' Mesa Petroleum. That year also brought a new term to the deal lexicon: Pac-Man defense—used to describe a defensive tactic where the target of a hostile offer bids for its suitor. Bendix found itself the victim of such a defense by Martin-Marietta after it had launched its own hostile bid for the latter. In the end, Bendix was acquired in a white knight rescue by Allied Corporation. All of these situations meant one thing for the arbitrageur: opportunity. The frequency of bidding wars was obviously a boon to the community. As the decade progressed, both the risk arbitrage and M&A businesses would be shaped by the opposing forces of the Drexel money machine and, on the legislative side, the counterweight of antitakeover legislation.

One of the more onerous developments of the 1980s was the widespread adoption of the "poison pill" takeover defense. In upholding the pill, the Delaware Superior Court essentially sanctioned a device that would for years impair the rights of shareholders to receive a fair price from a suitor deemed unfriendly by a sitting management. The obvious conflict between this new antitakeover defense and the basic rights of shareholders was, and is to this day, inexplicably lost on the Delaware courts. Adopted by a simple board resolution, the poison pill had the effect of a charter amendment without shareholder approval. The basic concept behind a poison pill was to dilute the voting power of a hostile shareholder by disallowing its shareholder's equal participation in a discount stock issue that would be triggered by the raider crossing a stated percentage shareholding threshold. In the 1985 case of

Moran v. Household International, the Delaware Supreme Court rejected a request by Moran to strike down Household's poison pill. This historic decision solidified the presence of an antidemocratic takeover device that, regrettably, continues to undermine shareholder rights. The stock market crash of 1987 was the defining event of the decade and brought the first major macroeconomic shock to the arb community. Since, at the time, most of the high-profile announced deals were for cash consideration, the arbitrageur lacked the short side, which, when moving in tandem with the long, insulates a position from day-to-day market movements. Spreads widened so sharply on that historic day that the entire arb community suffered significant losses. The question in the immediate aftermath of the crash was, what's next? Opinions varied on the future of the risk arbitrage business, as the financing of mergers and acquisitions business itself hinges on investors' appetite for risk. Some firms elected to close their arbitrage operations entirely, while others, seeing a quick end to what they believed was simply an index arbitrage meltdown, elected to extend additional credit lines to their arb desks. The idea was to capitalize on the drastically oversold market conditions and mispriced spreads brought on by the panic selling. Those firms that withstood the panic profited handsomely, as the market stabilized under the watchful eye of the Federal Reserve, spreads narrowed, and the naysayers were proven wrong. Only one year later, in fact, KKR, armed with Drexel's war chest, won a bidding war and acquired RJR for $25 billion in the largest LBO to date.

A two-year respite from the 1987 turmoil was shattered in 1989 with the catastrophic collapse of the $300-per-share, union-led buyout of UAL. If the October 1987 crash was the seminal event of the decade for the larger financial community, the UAL deal collapse was its counterpart for the arbitrageurs. Referred to in gallows humor as "United Arbitrage Liquidation," the UAL deal made tragically clear the meaning of "risk" in the risk arbitrage game. The one-day plunge in UAL's share price and the collateral damage from arb desks dumping positions to raise capital for margin calls sent the DJIA down a then-significant 190 points. UAL was a shining example of one of the many perils of an overheated market: the phenomenon of confidence overtaking caution, a time-tested recipe for disaster. With the benefit of hindsight, many an arb looked longingly at the prices of the out-of-the-money put options on UAL common stock just prior to the collapse. A simple married put strategy would have insulated every arb from the damage to their long positions. Instead, some arbs found themselves setting up their own shops as their benefactors shied away from the risk arb business entirely. The UAL deal, while a calamity in its own right, was also a symptom of a larger problem. The overleveraging and general excess that had for the better part of the decade consumed Wall Street was finally coming home to roost.

The decade that had brought so much innovation to the arbitrage community and M&A business, as well as to corporate America, was ending on a decidedly sour note. Suspicions that the junk bond market was beginning to live up to its name were exerting enormous pressure on Drexel's ability to sell new debt. The firm was suddenly rudderless without the presence of Michael Milken, who in 1988 had been indicted on 98 counts of fraud and racketeering. Drexel itself was busy fending off its own indictment from then New York Attorney General Rudy Giuliani, and the earlier insider trading scandals involving Ivan Boesky, Dennis Levine, and John Mulheren had begun to shape a somewhat villainous image of the arbitrageur. The predictions at the time were dire. Risk arbitrage itself appeared to be imperiled by the tribulations of its host, the M&A business, and, with a slowing economy raising fears of a recession, lighthearted Wall Street discussions of bidding wars gave way to more somber discussions of defaults and bankruptcies.

1990s

The early part of the next decade was a quiet period for the risk arbitrage business. The country was experiencing its first recession since 1982, and the job cuts and retrenchment within corporate America had all but extinguished the heady feel of the "go-go" eighties. Drexel Burnham in 1990 officially ended its reign as the premiere bond house on Wall Street when a series of credit rating downgrades forced it from the commercial paper market and into bankruptcy proceedings. The speed with which the junk bond powerhouse had risen to prominence and then vanished was stunning. The rest of corporate America was coping with the debt hangover of the 1980s and the junk bond market, which once dominated conversation on Wall Street, was in ruins.

With the absence of an active deal market, spreads on announced deals suffered. The thinning of the arbitrage community had been more than offset by the scarcity of deals. This left the remaining arbs chasing few opportunities and doing so for lower returns. What followed was a movement by some firms into distressed arbitrage. In an attempt to capitalize on the rash of defaults and bankruptcies, some arbitrage departments turned their attention to valuing the outstanding debt of those companies that were facing restructuring. The idea was to then position their firm's capital in the debt of those companies in the hope of recovering a larger payout than a panicky bond market was anticipating. While this business was popular with some in the community, many arbs stood their ground, concerned by the lack of liquidity in some of the debt issues and viewing the heavy component of bankruptcy law as well as the new structure of analysis as an imprudent stretch from their classical training. As the economy recovered, the risk arb business was again given life by the new catchphrases of corporate America: scale and global positioning. Corporations were finding that the needs for scale within industries and indeed across continents were again pushing them toward the consolidation game.

After the drought, the arbs were ready. The mid- and late 1990s saw a wave of consolidation amid a tech boom that transformed the productivity of corporations on a scale not seen since the industrial revolution. It appeared that American CEOs had concluded that it was simply easier to purchase market share than to grow it organically, and they had at their disposal the perfect currency: their own stock. The rise in equity prices throughout the 1990s was the same boon to stock deals as the availability of junk bond financing was to the cash deals of the 1980s. As in most economic rebounds, CEOs were finding that out of the wreckage of recession, they and their competitors were emerging with leaner balance sheets and attractive stock valuations. The newly expanding economy provided the impetus to adjust to a more aggressive growth focus, and the deal machine was once again in high gear.

One of the notable developments of the decade involved the resilience of the poison pill and its ability to shelter boards using the "just-say-no" defense. The development was the increasing objection to the device by shareholders. The targets of two closely followed hostile deals faced a new element—organized shareholder resistance. In 1995, Moore Corp. launched a hostile offer for Wallace Computer. Wallace adopted the standard "just-say-no" defense and relied on its poison pill for protection. Moore Corp. petitioned the Delaware Federal court to strike down Wallace's antitakeover defenses, namely the pill. Moore withdrew its offer after its petition failed and the pill was upheld, but not before Wallace found itself the target of a shareholder proposal to amend the company's bylaws so that its takeover defenses would terminate 90 days after a qualified offer had been received by the company. This event was one step in what became a turning point in the attitudes of shareholders toward recalcitrant boards. The "just-say-no" defense was now being reconsidered as an acceptable measure. What had been sanctioned by the Delaware courts was now coming under fire by popular revolt. The issue was again in focus in 1997 when the board of Pennzoil rejected a cash and stock offer from UPR. While the board consistently argued that the offer was too low, the real impediment was the company's poison pill and the prospect of costly litigation that it promised. After failing to bring Pennzoil's board to the negotiating table, UPR did in fact withdraw its offer, citing a deterioration in the value of Pennzoil's assets. To the arb, it appeared more likely that the poison pill was the real culprit. While victorious in the end, Pennzoil, too, found itself the target of a shareholder revolt in the form of a proposal to elect a dissident director to the board and a demand for sweeping changes to the company's governance of change-of-control situations. It was becoming clear that by the late nineties, shareholders were no longer willing to accept a board's refusal to allow them to judge the fairness of an offer. Shareholders wanted their say as owners, and their relationship to a board of directors was changing forever.

The arbitrage business continued to feel the influx of new players as it was being seen by increasing numbers of people as an attractive use of capital. The compression of spreads continued, but by the late 1990s, the proliferation of derivatives was bringing pressure from a new direction. Spreads were being compressed not only by the volume of players but also by the margin that they employed. Arbitrage positions were now being taken by way of simple collateral deposits on derivative contracts, rather than through the actual purchase of common stock. The result was an amount of leverage that allowed arbs who were using these methods to profitably play spreads that appeared too thin for a profitable return. This action further squeezed the profit that was available by playing the deals through the common stock and began to raise the issue of whether the "risk" in risk arbitrage was being mispriced.

2000s

The first decade began in a manner reminiscent of some of the difficulties faced in the early nineties. In this instance, the aftermath of a speculative boom in Internet and technology stocks that had distorted both the traditional risk/reward expectations of investors, as well as the historical price-to-earnings multiples of entire sectors of the market, had utterly poisoned market sentiment. It was a period marked by the brutal and seemingly endless destruction of wealth that had been created in the dot-com boom of the late 1990s. A new distrust of corporate management, sown by the accounting scandals at Enron and WorldCom, as well as by the complete collapse of the Internet stocks, was now deeply rooted in both Wall and Main streets. CEOs were now being required, for the first time, to certify their company's financial reports in writing. The performance of the equity markets reflected a nation of investors disenchanted by corporate malfeasance. The revelations were beginning to make the explosive equity returns of the 1990s look, in hindsight, like nothing more than a shell game. Gone were the days when a technology company's CEO could entice the shareholders of a target company with the implied promise of two- or three-fold gains in the combined company's stock price. The folly of Internet stocks was being driven home even at staid, blue-chip corporations like Time Warner, which, in one of the most glaring examples of poor judgment in corporate history, had accepted AOL common stock in the two companies' much-touted 2001 merger. The arbitrageur in those days was wise to maintain a full hedge, for while the deals were still being churned out by optimistic investment bankers, the risk of a collapse in an acquirer's stock price could have been lethal. What has defined the current decade more than any development in the arbitrage or investment banking field are the changes in the relationship of shareholders to their fiduciaries at publicly traded corporations.

What in the 1970s and 1980s might have been described as a "rogue shareholder" was now operating under the label "activist." What started in the 1990s as revolts against entrenched managements that had ignored their shareholders in rejecting high premium offers from unwanted suitors was now an institution. Funds designed specifically for the purpose of engaging managements to enhance shareholder value were raising capital at an astonishing pace. The new idea was to establish a position in shares of an underperforming company and then present a solution, in the form of a new business plan, to management. In prior years, resistance had been common; the old "just-say-no" defense was still prevalent in boardrooms, and the spirit of it had been used successfully against shareholders who wished to voice their concerns. The current decade brought a widespread change to attitudes regarding a shareholder's voice. Perhaps the distrust of management had given way to a new willingness to demand, publicly, better performance from management. Activists, although still not genuinely welcome in the boardroom, were now warmly greeted by both the press and the investment community. Hedge funds, unencumbered by the investment banking ties of their larger competitors, were free to voice their opinions without the fear of a backlash from a parent company or an investment banking division fearful of losing its next underwriting fee. Activist funds were, in increasing numbers, succeeding in gaining board seats, and pushing agendas that ranged from changes to administrative governance frameworks, to more aggressive plans such as restructurings and even mergers. The age of the activist had clearly arrived. Once the low-hanging fruit at poorly managed US corporations had been picked, activists turned their attention to Continental Europe. European companies were, by comparison, decades behind their Western counterparts in the area of corporate governance. Equally archaic, however, were their attitudes toward shareholder's rights. The specter of a fund manager challenging a board of directors at a shareholder meeting was appalling to European managements and even to some of their large shareholders. The activist needed to plan a careful approach to avoid losing a public relations battle before his ideas were even on the table. As the decade progressed, even European managements began to adopt a more shareholder-friendly posture. European CEOs were recognizing that without reforms, their markets might be viewed as less efficient and therefore less competitive. Without efficiency, they might fail to attract capital from the international community. While the European business community has begun to change its attitudes toward active shareholders, the political establishment, particularly in Germany and France, continues to object to the participation of these funds in the management of public companies, on the grounds that they have no long-term interest in the companies themselves, or in the economies of the countries in which they invest. During the recent political season in Germany, for example, activists were labeled as "locusts" in an attempt to paint them, for political purposes of course, as the enemy of the German worker. The absurdity of this argument has not been lost on business leaders. Many have publicly cautioned their elected officials about the economic perils of appearing unwilling to embrace a more modern management philosophy that is inclusive of all ideas to enhance value. The activist battles between shareholders and managements in both the United States and Europe will undoubtedly continue for years to come. Any movement within the business community that has as its purpose the efficient management of a corporation's assets is unlikely to be derailed. Surely there will be mistakes and periods of backlash against aggressive shareholders, but the essential elements of the activist movement are here to stay.

One can examine the field of active value investing in terms that are quite familiar to the arbitrageur. It is possible to identify what is, in a sense, the spread in these situations. For each activist target, there is a current market price, which can be seen as reflecting the performance of the current management. A research department may then analyze the potential values of the corporation's assets under an array of restructuring scenarios and arrive at a target price, which, to a classically trained arbitrageur, might be the activist equivalent of a bid price under a traditional takeover scenario. The difference between the current market price and the anticipated values under each restructuring scenario can be considered "the spread." The spread could be captured in the event that the restructuring succeeds. An arbitrageur who commits capital to such a situation is taking both the risk that the proposal is accepted and that the proposal is sound. The time frame is, of course, considerably longer than the traditional risk arbitrage scenario, as it may require a full meeting cycle or longer for even the successful activist to implement a new agenda. What might be called "active arbitrage" is a demanding endeavor. Some investors from the arbitrage community elect to participate silently in the projects of other activists, while others are using their expertise in valuing corporations under restructuring scenarios, as well as their extensive knowledge of change-of-control scenarios and the attendant tactics associated with them, to initiate activist agendas themselves. Few professional investors, in fact, are better qualified to navigate the unique obstacles of corporate activism than the classically trained risk arbitrageur. The still-developing field of activism may hold great promise for those who honed their skills during the takeover wars of past decades.

11. ARBITRAGE TO ACTIVISM—MY JOURNEY BEGINS

My father retired in 1971, and I took over. As I mentioned, with Clark Clifford's high recommendation to Bache & Co chairman, John Leslie my challengers to the position were quickly overcome. From that point on, I had a sterling record. But I found it not as challenging or as interesting as I thought I would. All you're effectively doing in "risk" arbitrage is passively taking a risk in merger proposals because there's always a spread in between the proposed price and the market price, which is reflective of the inherent risk. What you're really doing is sitting on your prayer rug every morning, wishing and praying these things go through because they're always going to get

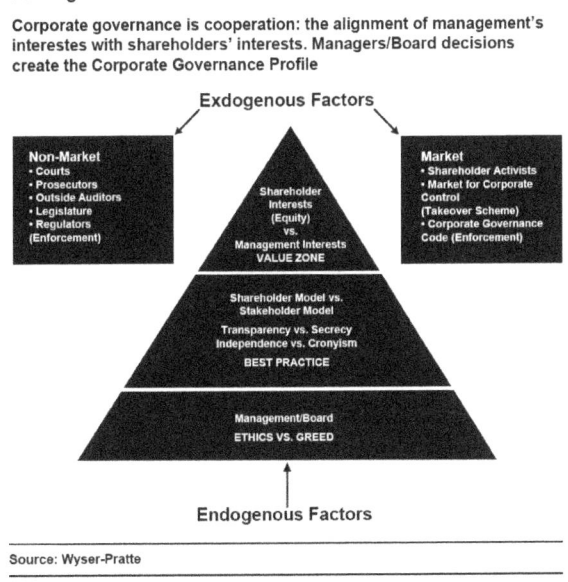

I created this value pyramid to demonstrate how the conflicts are pictured and how value is created at the top of the pyramid by dealing with shareholder interests rather than management interests in the "value zone."

attacked by antitrust agencies, unhappy shareholders, or one thing or another. A lot of these deals don't go through, so you have to very carefully select the ones that you invest in. I found that I'd rather make my own fate, which fits with the theme of this book—if I take an activist role in a situation where there is a large differential between the market price and the restructured price of a target, that's much more interesting, and I can dictate the outcome by my intervention as an activist. That's why I started to shift into activist strategies. Buying stock and having no influence on its price is not much more than gambling at the track.

> A little French humor, apparently at my expense, but I think they were spot on.

"J'ai une tactique: celle du chameau qui met son nez sous la bache. Une fois qu'il a mis on nez sous la bache, les entourloupes cessent."
- Guy Wyser-Pratte

"I have a tactic: that of the camel that sticks its nose under the tent flap. Once it has put its nose under the tent flap, the tricks cease."
- Guy Wyser-Pratte

The first activist deal I did was in 1974; we had accumulated in my arbitrage department a large position in the preferred shares of Great Western United, which was the holding company for Great Western Sugar, one of the major sugar refiners in the United States. When the sugar price shot through the roof, they had lots of money with which to pay off their preferred arrears.

For those unfamiliar with these structures, preferred dividends in arrears are unpaid, cumulative dividends owed to preferred shareholders that must be paid before any dividends can be distributed to common shareholders. These preferred shares were deeply in arrears, so we accumulated a large position in the preferred shares, which meant we had the right to collect on the unpaid dividends. Naturally, I was, at this time, incentivized to reach out via a letter to the chairman of Great Western United—a maverick by the name of Billy White, who used to run around Denver on his bicycle—and what I said was, "It's time for you to pay off your preferred dividends." To which Mr. White said, "No, we're not going to do that." To which I said, "Are you absolutely sure?" To which he responded, "Yes!" Well, as I am sure you have assumed by now, we filed a suit in the Delaware Chancery Court—which is where everybody headquarters due to their well-established corporate legal framework, specialized court system for business disputes, and favorable tax conditions—and lo and behold, a week after I filed the lawsuit with a partner at L. F. Rothschild (another arbitrage firm that also had a large position in the preferred chairs), we got a check in the mail for the entire amount of the preferred arrears.

This was to my greatest surprise and exaltation. I was so impressed with what had happened that it immediately triggered an epiphany that would set us on a brand-new course. "Aha," I said, "there's something in standing up to these folks. You stand your ground, and if you're right, you can prevail." That was the catalytic moment that started me off on the road to activism. I did it on behalf of Bache, then Pru-Bache, and then, when I went on my own, in 1991, I was no longer restricted by the constraints of my fellow directors. I was, by that time, a director of Bache & Co. and the board would get a little bit upset with me at times for going after people like McGraw-Hill or Gerber Baby products, to name a few.

Gerber was one of the great ones, and again, I learned a lesson. You take the microphone when it's given to you in order to address the annual meeting of shareholders, and you start blasting the management. Until they literally grab the microphone away from you. That is where you get the support of the press—which, I reiterate, is one of the key elements of activism. In all, about 101 initiatives in shareholder activism that those forty volumes of clippings in my office reflect. Certain press stories, such as the London School of Business—which I will link to at the end of this chapter—researched who was the most active activist at the time. Not surprisingly, it was yours truly. It was not long before people saw the success I was having and followed me in the pursuit of activism the way they had followed me when I wrote the book on arbitrage. Nobody had ever written about these things before. It's not like you could just Google it. If there was no book, you had to have lunch with people like me to learn the secrets.

What drives me is a belief that the world deserves to know what drives this activity. How does one make money in it? When I shared that in my first book, everybody became an arbitrageur, and when I decided to go and launch activism, everybody wanted to become shareholder activists.

In 2007, I was given an award by Alternative Investment News Digest for Fund Manager of the Year because of the two strategies that I had developed. It's not that I invented these strategies, but I had certainly developed them, and through my leveraging of the press, I had been credited with much of the activity. Activism is really just an accelerator for risk arbitrage because you're active in the spread. The spreads become smaller when you can influence corporate governance. Less time on the prayer rug and more time pushing the management to do the right thing. But what is the right thing? It can be harder to see from the inside when you are blinkered by internal issues at hand. From the outside it can be far easier to identify strategies that can affect desired change. Divesting defunct subsidiaries, ending non-profitable partnerships, and generally improving or creating competitive strategy.

One of the key instruments we use is convincing management that they aren't earning their cost of capital in various subsidiaries. This is an investing strategy very popular in the United States developed by a group called Stern Stewart. They invented the EVA (Economic Value Added) strategies, and their view always was that if a company is not earning its cost of capital, they shouldn't be in that business. A good example of when we successfully employed this strategy was IWKA in Germany when we went after them in 2003. We were able to hold the management's feet to the fire who promised to get rid of non-producing subsidiaries in order to clean up their balance sheet. I warned them in 2003 and in 2004 that if they didn't do it within a set time limit, I was going to go after them in a proxy fight. They didn't take my threat seriously, so I launched the proxy fight. The next thing you know, the president had to resign, we kicked out the board, we moved in a whole new management slate, got rid of all the unprofitable subsidiaries, and the company became one of the premier companies in the world in robotics: KUKA ROBOTS. Unfortunately, a Beijing-based company bought this company because they wanted to be a big manufacturer of robots in China. It was one of those things that I tried to block, but I didn't always win. I went to Bundeskartellamt (BKartA)—the German Federal Cartel Office, Germany's national competition regulatory agency—which is headquartered in Bonn. I went to the European Commission, where Chris Patten was a senior official. I went to CFIUS—the Committee on Foreign Investment in the United States—and told them that the Chinese had no business owning this company because it was involved in certain areas of defense. We did succeed in having CFIUS force KUKA to sell the branch that makes arresting gear for aircraft carriers when the planes land. But despite all my efforts, we failed in blocking the Chinese from buying the company. They paid a big price, so, of course, everybody wanted to cash in. Angela Merkel, who was then Chancellor of Germany, was asked what she felt about this, to which she said, "Well, now that this has gone through, maybe we should change the law." I was dumbfounded. The horse had well left the barn. One of the pearls of German engineering had been sold to our enemy, and it wasn't the only one that had been sold at that time.

It is the nature of activism that leads us to get involved in these international and geopolitical realms. For instance, I went after the big German defense company, Rheinmetall AG—now the biggest in Europe. At the time, their stock was very low, and they were seeking outside financing, which they couldn't do because the stock price was too low. I went to talk to the managers and the chairman in Germany, and we decided to work together to get the price up. Again, the stock went rocketing up, and they implemented a few of the changes that we worked out together, and they were just deliriously happy with me. The chairman was Werner Engelhardt. One day he called me and said, "Can I come see you in New York? I have another target for you, it's called IWKA. They're worth three times what they're selling for." And that is how the IWKA deal came about. It's a small world when you're talking risk arbitrage activism. Word of mouth goes a long way in this field.

We had great success in France. I finished up with a tally of 37 companies in France after having been invited over there to do what I do. We went after the Taittinger Group, which is the champagne maker. They also owned a lot of different assets: Louvre hotels, Baccarat Crystal, Annick Goutal perfume shops, and the like. In a period of two or three years, we quadrupled the stock. The French establishment was not happy with my doing this, but the French shareholder population was deliriously happy with me because we pushed up the price of the shares two, three, and four times their original.

My first big transaction in France was called Stratfor-Facom, comprised of two very different businesses: household appliances and a great hand tools business. Unfortunately, its CEO was Henri Lachmann, a very political and influential animal and a member of the French "copinage," or "good old boys" club.

I went public after taking a 5% position in 1996, pushing them to separate their two unrelated businesses. In France, it's not about economic or stock market efficiency; it's about control of masses of assets, so the resistance was fierce. Lachmann put the authorities on our backs. The AMF called me in for the first of many interviews and had La Brigade Financière rifle through the apartments of my Paris colleagues, looking for documents. None to be found.

Finally, I wound up in front of a panel of three women judges on a false charge of defamation, which in France is as common as a parking ticket. I tried to be charming with these three elderly ladies, smiling seductively like Giancarlo Giannini at the Nazi POW camp commander in the 1976 hilarious movie *Seven Beauties*. It didn't work for him either. The judges had already been gotten to and fined me 10k Francs. No big deal, but a mark against me.

So, how did it turn out with Strafor-Facom? Despite all the howling, they split the company into two parts, both of which were swallowed up by acquisitors, just as I had suggested would happen. Lachmann was then appointed head of Schneider Electric S.A., a much bigger company, where he sojourned from 2006 to 2015. He had gained handsomely from my intervention into his prior time at Strafort.

Then in 2001, I had a run-in with the new head of the COB—forerunner to the AMF. I arranged an appointment with its president, Gérard Rameix, to show him evidence I had garnered on an adversary. He listened attentively to my story, and then asked, "So what, Monsieur Wyser-Pratte, do YOU intend to do about it?" To which I replied, "Monsieur Rameix, it is not my job to investigate such matters. You are the gendarme of financial fraud. It is your job. Additionally, I have mostly done your job for you!"

I can recall his face turning a very bright shade of red. End of interview. But from that moment on, he was onto me like Chief Inspector Javert from *Les Misérables*, forever hounding the resistance fighter, Jean Valjean.

In 2010, when I set my sights on Lagardère, it was the beginning of an increasing crescendo of harassment and attacks from the French authorities. They manufactured an insider trading case against me and arranged for two convicted felons to give false depositions to the authorities. The authorities accepted their word over mine, even with all my credentials and track record. I followed my standard modus operandi of active investing, of studying a situation, seeing if I could do something about improving the price, taking a position, announcing it, working with the press, and so on. As a result, I was sanctioned by the French Sanctions Commission: La Commission des Sanctions, which is part of the AMF—the French SEC.

At the entrance to this Commission was a notice with the day's scheduled hearings, upon which my name appeared. Coincidentally, on those steps was my good friend and collaborator, Pierre-Henri Leroy, president of Proxinvest. Pierre-Henri happened to glance at these noticed hearings. At the same moment, my aforementioned pursuer, Gérard Rameix, entered the scene. The two knew each other well.

"Why is my friend Guy's name on this list?" Asked Pierre-Henri.

"Oh, he is a terrible, evil inside trader." Responded Rameix.

"Don't be ridiculous. I have invited Guy on a river cruise to address our institutional clients about his experiences in France." Pierre-Henri stated, graciously.

After this sanction, I informed Pierre-Henri that I didn't want to embarrass him with his client base abroad, so I reluctantly withdrew. Pierre-Henri understood.

So, they fined me €1,300,000. I had made around €300,000 for my clients over a short period of time on a market-to-market basis. To this day—I've held the stock for almost 15 years now—I never sold a single share. Not the sign of an inside trader. But, c'est la vie.

Somebody who's trading on inside information buys stock, and after the information hits, he's out. I mean, the proof is in the pudding in this thing. After the Sanctions Commission, I had to go through the Appeals Court of Paris, the Supreme Court of France, the Court of Human Rights in Strasbourg, the European Commission in Brussels, and the Ombudsman for the European Commission, and then I found out about the forces working against me. The European Commission was working with us to get a favorable decision through a "letter of Closure," which would have allowed me to reopen the case in France, but they threw me under the bus because Thierry Breton, who was a Commissioner and the only French Commissioner at the Commission—a real scumbag—was told to get me nixed by the French authorities. He lobbied his fellow commissioners hard, unbeknown to me at the time. I found out only recently how hard he had worked against me in lobbying all the other commissioners. I have emails showing that the Commission was working with me to give me the language that would have solved my case, but that's not what happened. They threw me under the bus and didn't even send me the opinion. They sent it through some other channel to somebody else, who sent it to me. There was some real skulduggery going on there, and I only found out about it a few months ago. Fifteen years on, and I am still fighting to clear my name from this ridiculous charge. In a way, this injustice has burdened me and bogged me down for a decade and a half. It has cost me, in defending myself, as much as the penalty that I would have had to pay, which I haven't paid to this day, nor will I ever. I am planning on a new approach I can take to finally get justice from the French. I'm just not through trying to reverse the situation, and this may be the missing piece that I needed, along with the letter from François Gontier, the "smoking gun," that nobody at the Commission and notably Ûgo Bassi of DG 15, can locate.

To go from the sublime to the ridiculous, I had subsequently, in May 2023, filed a "Requête en Revision" with the AMF to review my case. I had annexed a letter from my DC attorney, Paul Leder—former head of the SEC'S International Division—outlining the hardships that the AMF decision had inflicted upon me. I also attached an affidavit from the former president of EEM, the "smoking gun" letter, which represented that their was no inside information to transmit to me during the time period in controversy. This same affidavit was provided to the European Commission which, mysteriously, they have been unable to locate. Either attachment sufficed to have the case reviewed by the AMF. Two years hence, I have not had the courtesy of a response from the AMF.

There have been many articles written about this case over the years, one of which is particularly poignant. Published in 2013 on a French news site (linked via QR code below) was an article that raised one of the most important issues. The article begins, "This is a major blow for Guy Wyser-Pratte. The financial buccaneer has just been fined €1.3 million by the AMF for insider trading in the Electricité et Eaux de Madagascar affair." It goes on to say that it is particularly surprising that the AMF gave credence to the accusations of the trio of bunglers who brought Guy Wyser-Pratte before the French financial regulator. His accusers: François Gontier, Frédéric Doulcet, and Marc Bognon, whose successive contradictory statements ultimately led the AMF to make this astonishing decision were also sentenced to heavy fines, respectively. Scan the QR code to read the original article.

There is no question it can be a gut-wrenching business. That's why I decided I wanted to do something where I could control the outcome, at least to some extent. When I started with activism, my father had one comment that he used to make to me when watching me work with the press, etc. He'd say, "Captains Courageous," referring to the book by Rudyard Kipling. "Why do you think you're such a big shot? You can make all these big public statements." To which I would say, "Hey, you're talking to somebody who was a Company Commander in the United States Marines. They don't teach you to be shy." He accepted that.

Another activist initiative I undertook in 1987 saved me, if not all of Wall Street. Nobody knows about this episode. On Monday, October 19, 1987, another huge market crash occurred due to a perfect storm. The three heads of the storm were program trading, portfolio insurance, and the icing on the cake that brought it all down was Rostenkowski's (Chairman, House Ways and Means) interest rate deduction bill. People on Wall Street thought it was triggered by the failure of the buyout of United Airlines. Many professionals blamed it on "program trading," which created waves of selling through the NYSE's supercomputers that triggered the sale of massive amounts of stock. What started the cascade of selling was the leveraged buyout of United. Because of the proposed bill, the financing was unavailable.

If you know what the cause is of such a market move, you know the off-ramp. I knew the culprit. The chairman of the House Ways and Means Committee—Dan Rostentowski—had introduced a bill in the House of Representatives proposing to eliminate the deductibility of interest on acquisition loans when half of the listed companies on the New York Stock Exchange were trading on the basis of their ascribed takeover premiums. Any takeovers would be debt-financed, so interest deductibility was critical for these presumptive mergers to see the light of day. All said shares were thus collapsing and creating the market panic.

I had noticed this proposed regulation in the House of Representatives. I sent an envoy into Rostentowski's meeting room with a large sign saying, Rostentowski's anti-interest rate deductions bill is causing the stock market crash. He was indeed causing the crash due to his interest rate proposal. The next day, he withdrew his bill, and the market started to recover, and fully regained its posture in a matter of weeks. I, in the meantime, with malice and forethought, had correctly analyzed the fault line in the markets, and when the Chairman, George Ball, came down to ask my opinion, I explained to him the unfolding cause and proposed to double my positions at the low point of the market. Ball even gave me an extra line of credit to throw the dice. It worked!

I can't say I see a similar off-ramp for Trump's ill-conceived reciprocal tariff impositions, which have caused a $6 trillion sell-off in US markets. The only savior for this is if rational Republicans in the Senate lean on Trump and his cabinet of lightweights to reverse course on these tariffs. If not, we are back to the Hawley–Smoot Tariff of 100 years ago, which caused the Great Depression. Elon Musk has proposed a positive solution: zero tariffs across the board within a free-trade zone comprising North America and Europe. That would work, I believe.

In the meantime, several of Trump's front billionaires, plus Treasury Secretary Bissent, have warned Trump that the collapsing bond market was a signal of impending doom for the world economy. Suffice it to say, Trump blinked, restructuring tariff rates to aim primarily at China, and the markets' slide has been temporarily interrupted. Qui vivra vera!—whatever will be will be, or time will tell.

Through all these ups and downs, however, I have prided myself on doing the right thing. You are not always treated kindly for doing what's right, as there is often somebody else trying to protect their "derrière." For example, I left Prudential-Bache in 1991. My exit was not at all what you would call smooth. In fact, the whole story has made it into other books. One such book is the *Serpent on the Rock* by Kurt Eichenwald. We will explore the demise of Prudential-Bache in the next chapter.

Throughout my business life, I have been labeled a corporate raider, but the evidence says otherwise. Actually, my work is the antithesis of that term and is best described as activism. Actively working to improve shareholder and, therefore, my own holdings' value. To do that, I always leveraged the press, which is why I have over 40 volumes of press clippings lined up in my office. I kept everything, and it documents a fascinating and detailed portrayal of a lifetime spent in a very specialized field. Far more than can be shared in this one memoir. But I am drawing on those records to highlight the highs and lows of a career that I have richly enjoyed, for the most part. I have heard many times people speak of Wall Street as a soulless void that doesn't create anything; it just takes, parasitically, from what others create. But what I have done is always endeavor to uncover, create, and increase value by activism. No executive board, with genuine good intentions for the company they oversee, should ever lament my involvement. Of course, there are always agendas, which are quickly revealed if a board does not have shareholder value front and center.

But for activism to succeed, you need the press. After a few successful initiatives, the press gets hungry for adventure and is always interested to investigate, "What is this Guy up to now?" they would say. Leveraging the press to increase the value of a company by public perception is the most important tool in the corporate activist's arsenal. After, of course, the ability to identify the potential upside in any scenario. Sometimes boards don't see it, and that can certainly create friction and hostility. But, for the most part, if I appear on the scene, it is cause for shareholder celebration, if I do say so myself.

After establishing a foundational track record, we were able to analyze "the activism effect"—the immediate stock price movement when we announce that we're involved in a situation. Measuring from the day that we announced to a week or so afterward, the average price of a share had improved by 15–18% on most of the transactions that we were involved in, simply because we had established credibility. Our involvement created sentiment—the perception of value even before any had been created—and that encouraged co-investment, which manifests as further stock price increases and the rising price of the market.

Another of my secret tools of arbitrage activism is a military strategy called maneuver warfare. It is well-articulated in a book called *The Marine Corps Way—Using Maneuver Warfare to Lead a Winning Organization*—by Jason A. Santamaria, which I helped write.

In the book, Santamaria presents the model as a strategic approach for overcoming resistance—whether on a battlefield or in a business setting—by coordinating multiple complementary capabilities to overwhelm and disorient the opposition. It's a key principle borrowed from the Marine Corps' doctrine of maneuver warfare.

The central idea is that no single method of attack is sufficient against a well-defended or resistant target. Instead, by applying multiple, distinct lines of effort in a synchronized fashion, you force the target into a no-win situation. If they defend against one type of pressure, they expose themselves to another.

In Military Terms: In combat, this might mean using infantry, armor (tanks), artillery, and air power together so that an enemy defending against one becomes vulnerable to the others. For example:

- If an enemy hides from airstrikes in bunkers, they become vulnerable to ground forces.
- If they fight the infantry directly, they're exposed to aerial attack or artillery fire.

This creates a dilemma—any choice they make leads to disadvantage.

In Business Terms (as adapted in the book): In organizational leadership, a "combined arms" approach means using multiple levers of influence or strategies at once—so that resistance from stakeholders, competitors, or employees is met from several angles.

Example Applications:
- **Strategic change initiative:** You combine clear top-down leadership (command presence), peer-to-peer influence (culture change), structural incentives (rewards or re-orgs), and grassroots buy-in (employee engagement efforts).
- **Competitive market strategy:** A company might simultaneously launch a new product, adjust pricing, ramp up marketing, and introduce a customer loyalty program—making it hard for a competitor to counter all aspects at once.

The Goal: To disorient and outmaneuver resistance, rather than trying to overpower it directly. The resistance becomes ineffective not because it is crushed head-on, but because it's outflanked and outpaced by a broader, multidimensional approach.

I have other weapons, but you get the idea: An outside influence, unburdened by politics, internal scuffles, or personal agendas, brings strategic vision with military execution to bear, and positive effects are inevitable. Smart leadership brings agents of change such as this into organizations under the banner of strategy execution consultants or cultural transformation experts.

Arbitrage to Activism—My Journey Begins | **67**

I simply do it for the shareholders, and I put skin in the game. A self-funded mercenary, if you will.

Scan the QR code to view the London Business School Center for Corporate Governance document which shows Wyser-Pratte as the number one activist in Europe.

12. PRUDENTIAL-BACHE—A TALE AS OLD AS TIME

Throughout this chapter I will reflect on thoughts and events outlined in the book *Serpent on the Rock—Backstabbing. Lying. Embezzling, Cover-ups. Just Another Day on Wall Street in History's Biggest Corporate Swindle*—by Kurt Eichenwald. In addition, the book *In Good Faith* by Kathleeen Sharp is a well-researched, insightful analysis of the events that took place. For more depth, I encourage you to read these titles, but in regard to my involvement, here is my synopsis of those heavy-hearted days.

I always had my ear to the ground. As head of risk arbitrage at Bache, that was my job—watching tickers, reading signals, and catching rumors before they became headlines. That's how I first caught wind of something strange in 1978. Large blocks of Bache shares were moving, quietly but with purpose. I dug around and got a name: the Belzbergs. Canadian corporate raiders with a reputation.

It didn't take long before Jacobs, our ever-nervous chairman, called me from Munich in a panic. "Who are they?" he asked. I told him what I knew: they were serious, aggressive, and possibly dangerous.

Jacobs went white. "Terrible," he kept repeating, as if saying it would make it less true. Over the next few weeks, he obsessed over the Belzbergs—rightly so, as they crossed the 5% ownership threshold and filed with the SEC. He turned to Marty Lipton again for help, the same lawyer who saved us during the Tsai affair. But this time, Lipton was conflicted—he represented the Belzbergs.

I watched Jacobs spiral. I'd seen it before in other CEOs during takeover threats, but it was never easy to watch it from the inside. He panicked. We all did, in our own way.

Meanwhile, the Belzbergs played it smooth. Lipton arranged a meeting in L.A., and Sam Belzberg agreed not to buy more stock in exchange for a board seat. A clean, quiet deal. Or so it seemed.

When Belzberg flew to New York to meet "the boys on Gold Street," he got the runaround. Instead of a board seat, he got lunch at the Racquet and Tennis Club. Just him and Virgil Sherrill, the recently appointed president of

70 | Cutting My Own Path

Bache. Nothing was said. No deal. No board seat. Just pleasantries. Belzberg left furious. When he stormed into Lipton's office demanding answers, the truth was clear: someone at Bache had torpedoed the agreement.

Belzberg gave us two weeks to fix it. We didn't. And he started buying again. By the fall of 1979, Belzberg's stake had grown to nearly 7%. Jacobs, desperate and out of moves, made a call to the richest family in America: the Hunts. They were oil tycoons, silver speculators, and—more importantly—longtime Bache clients. Jacobs asked them to help us by buying a large chunk of Bache stock. They agreed. For a moment, we had a lifeline.

The Hunts were different. Big, brash Texans with an appetite for risk. They were also cornering the world silver market. Through us. They bought contracts by the thousands and eventually demanded delivery. We facilitated it all—and lent them the money to keep going.

By early 1980, we'd lent the Hunts $233 million. The silver market was overheated, and when it started to crack, the margin calls flooded in. The Hunts scrambled. We scrambled. Silver dropped fast—from $50 to the $20s in weeks. Then $10. Every dollar down brought us closer to collapse.

March 27, 1980. Silver fell to $10.80. Our exposure was catastrophic. We'd violated capital requirements. The SEC and NYSE descended on our offices. I was called out of a board meeting—someone wanted to buy the entire Hunt silver position. A Belgian firm. It was enough to keep us alive.

I ran back into the boardroom.

"We've got a bid!" I shouted.

I had gotten a call from Jean Peterbroeck—my host during my Brussels intern period and close personal friend—that Photogaevart, the Belgian film products producer, wanted to buy the lot. I had called Jean for help, seeing the firm could go under.

Relief spread like oxygen in a fire. We lived to fight another day. But we weren't safe. The banks came calling. They wanted more collateral on the loans we took to fund the Hunts. Sherrill faced them down. Elegant as always, he told them they'd get nothing more than the silver they'd already accepted. "Have a wonderful day," he said, and walked out.

Miraculously, we survived. We even posted a small profit that quarter thanks to Fred Horn's calm hand unwinding the Hunts' positions. But our victory was short-lived.

Prudential-Bache—A Tale as Old as Time | 71

The Hunts, in desperate need of cash, sold their Bache shares. And who do you think bought them? The Belzbergs. They were back—stronger than ever, with more than 15% of the firm. We had handed our enemies the keys.

When Jacobs met Belzberg again, he had nothing left to offer. No leverage. No allies. Only the weight of a collapsing firm and the ghost of a battle barely won. As for me, I stayed alert. The market never sleeps, and neither does a good arbitrageur. But I knew then that Bache's best days were behind it. We weren't just a firm under siege—we were a firm that had lost its way. And no amount of silver could buy it back.

By the early 1980s, the wheels were spinning faster than ever at Bache—deals, tax shelters, and Regulation D partnerships. Everyone was sprinting to keep up, and still we lagged behind. The tax shelter department, in particular, was drowning in work. New hires, interns, temps—anyone with a pulse and a pen was thrown into the fray.

I remember the name Lauren McNenney. She'd started as a temp with no financial experience, just an English major from Barnard. But in the frenzy, she became indispensable—editing brochures, logging financials, and even overseeing performance reports on energy deals. That's how far things had slipped: the monitoring work we bragged about to clients—the supposed oversight and due diligence—had been delegated to a summer temp who'd once been a lifeguard.

It was a farce. We presented ourselves as meticulous stewards of client money, but behind the curtain, it was patchwork and guesswork. Monitoring was a burden, not a priority—no fees in it, so no one wanted it. The firm was addicted to the next deal, the next commission, and keeping the gears turning, no matter how brittle the machinery underneath.

Even with all that, the real rot wasn't in operations. It was in leadership. After Prudential bought us, there was hope—real hope—that we could turn the corner. They had scale, capital, and credibility. But Bache couldn't help being Bache. We flubbed an acquisition of Bateman Eichler by announcing a deal before owning a meaningful stake—alerting the market and losing the firm to Kemper. Then we butchered the rollout of our big new product, the "Command Account," intended to challenge Merrill's cash management offering. Thousands of brochures were mis-mailed across the country. A client in Connecticut was told to open an account in Arizona. It was amateur hour.

From where I sat—watching stock movements and listening to the whispers behind closed doors—I could see it: Prudential was growing impatient. The only bright spot left was the tax shelter division. Darr and his people were printing money, riding the Reagan tax bill and Regulation D like a wave. But one success couldn't hide the sinking ship. Losses were mounting. In 1981, Bache earned $5 million on $730 million in revenue. The first months of 1982 were worse—bleeding millions. And Prudential was taking the hit. They weren't going to let it slide much longer.

Then came June. Jacobs, ever the optimist—or perhaps just deluded—hosted an anniversary breakfast to celebrate on year since the merger. He packed the cafeteria with executives, Prudential brass included. He gave a stiff speech, played a highlight reel of our "successes," and then, to everyone's horror, cued a clip from Annie.

There we sat, a roomful of Wall Street men, watching Albert Finney as Daddy Warbucks dance with a little redhead. The message was clear: Prudential was Daddy Warbucks, and we were the orphan they had adopted. And then, Jacobs—bless him—sang the last line himself: "I don't need anything but Pru."

You could hear the silence. It was a silence that screamed. I glanced at Howard Elisofon, sitting next to me. He leaned in and whispered, "Well, he's gonna be fired tomorrow." He wasn't far off.

Behind the scenes, Prudential was already preparing the coup. They'd hired headhunters months earlier to find a new CEO. Bache's losses, its mismanagement, the missed opportunities—it had all finally caught up. Harry Jacobs didn't know it, but the walls were already closing in.

They wanted a fixer. Someone who could bring order to chaos. All signs pointed to George Ball, the president of E.F. Hutton. He'd built Hutton into a retail powerhouse. Aggressive, disciplined, and already familiar with Bache—he'd been approached a year earlier and turned us down flat. But now? Now he was interested.

I'd heard whispers from the Street that Ball had grown tired of Hutton. The firm, for all its flash, was starting to wobble. He needed a lifeboat. And Bache, broken as it was, still had the bones of a real franchise.

By summer, Ball was in. Jacobs was out. The firm I'd joined—fast, hungry, fearless—was gone. What remained was bloated and brittle, clinging to pride and memory. We were an old lion limping off the battlefield, still growling but bleeding from too many wounds. And I? I kept watching the tape, reading the signs. That's what I'd always done. But by then, even I knew: the fall wasn't coming. It had already begun.

George Ball arrived like a thunderclap. Smooth, measured, but with a presence that made the walls straighten up. He wasn't loud, didn't bark orders, didn't need to. His reputation entered the building ten minutes before he did.

At Hutton, Ball had taken a clunky, underpowered retail brokerage and turned it into a juggernaut. Now, he had a new mandate: fix Bache—or bury it trying.

He started fast. No ceremonial breakfasts. No musical numbers. Just a parade of meetings and memos, each one with a clear tone: no more excuses, no more chaos, no more hiding behind the old name. I remember sitting across from him during one of our first strategy meetings. He didn't waste time on niceties. "You're the arb guy," he said. "Tell me who's going to try to kill us next." I liked him immediately.

Ball brought discipline to a place that had been running on fumes and fantasy. He tore through the bloated reporting lines, axed dead wood, and drilled into product profitability with the eye of a banker and the cynicism of a trader. For a while, it worked. Morale stabilized. The press began talking about a comeback. The Prudential people, once cringing in the shadows, started showing up to meetings with a little more swagger. But then the skeletons began falling out of the closet.

It turned out that Bache hadn't just been mismanaged. It had been overleveraged, overexposed, and, in some corners, utterly reckless. Our vaunted tax shelter division, which had been the golden child, came under scrutiny for its opaque structures and thin compliance practices. What had once looked like innovation now carried the scent of liability. And then there was silver.

Though we'd survived the Hunt disaster by a hair, we were still entangled in lawsuits and reputational damage. Clients and regulators were asking hard questions. Why had Bache extended so much credit? Why weren't risk controls stronger? Why had so many red flags been ignored?

Ball did his best to wall off the past, to put it all behind us. He rebranded the firm "Prudential-Bache," hoping the stability of the Prudential name would bleach away the mess of the past decade. But even a new name couldn't cover up the fatigue setting in. The brokers were restless, the clients were cautious, and the Street was watching.

We'd lost something fundamental—not just capital or credibility, but identity. In the 1960s and 1970s, Bache was a place that took bets, big ones. Sometimes they worked, sometimes they didn't—but there was an edge, a sharpness. It attracted sharp people. That edge had dulled. Ball tried to bring it back. He tried damn hard. But the firm wasn't built to be agile anymore. We were too big to pivot, too bruised to run.

I stayed on, running arbitrage, watching M&A flows, and listening for the next Belzberg, the next raid. But inside, I knew I was watching the sun set on something I'd once believed in.

One day in late 1983, I walked into the boardroom and caught sight of myself in the glass. Same suit, same routine—but the game had changed. We weren't playing to win anymore. We were playing to survive. And I don't play just to survive.

By 1985, the writing wasn't just on the wall—it was carved in stone. Prudential-Bache, despite George Ball's effort, had become an expensive lesson in overconfidence. We were still operating, still opening accounts, still handing out coffee mugs and glossy brochures—but the pulse was erratic.

Clients had long memories. Regulators too. Every quarter brought new settlements, new inquiries, and new reasons for the press to poke at old wounds. And the Street? The Street had moved on. Merrill was ascendant. Shearson had its swagger. Even Hutton, shaky as it was, had more momentum. We were no longer in the game. We were in the footnotes.

Ball, to his credit, tried to modernize us. He launched new products, cleaned up compliance, and pushed for better analytics. But it was like retrofitting an old battleship to fly. You could spend a fortune trying—but in the end, it's still a ship meant for a different era.

Then came the real shift. Behind closed doors, Prudential started floating the idea of a sale. First to investment banks. Then to regional players. Even a few international groups sniffed around. But no one wanted the whole thing—too much baggage, too many questions, too little future. Until Wachovia came knocking.

The Southern banking giant was looking to expand beyond its Carolina roots. Bache's retail network was wide, still staffed by some talented brokers. It was a decent fit—for them. For us, it was the final trade. We weren't being bought so much as absorbed.

The deal was announced in 1991, and by 1993, the name "Bache" was gone. Seventy years of history reduced to a footnote in Wachovia's quarterly report. Just like that, it was over. I didn't stay for the transition.

Looking back now, I see Bache for what it was—brilliant, chaotic, ambitious, flawed. It was a firm built on bold ideas and even bolder personalities. And for a long time, that was enough. But the world changed. Regulation tightened. Risk got priced differently. Markets became faster, colder, and more precise.

Bache never adjusted. We kept playing the old game in a new arena. And that's how you lose—not with a bang, but with a slow bleed. A missed deal here. A botched rollout there. A leader out of his depth singing show tunes while the floor gives way.

What stings isn't that we failed. It's that we could've succeeded. With the right leadership, with better discipline, with a little more humility and a little less hubris—we could've become something enduring. Instead, we became a cautionary tale.

I've carried that lesson into every boardroom since. Strategy matters. Governance matters. But the right people, with the right mindset, matter most. And if you're lucky—if you're really lucky—you'll know when to walk away before the music stops.

For me, that was the last great trade at Bache. Not a stock. Not a takeover. But the decision to step aside before history closed the book. They say Wall Street forgets quickly. But I haven't forgotten. I remember the ticker, the rumors, and the panicked calls from Vienna and Vancouver. I remember the arrogance and the blind spots. I remember the silver. And I remember the moment I knew it was time to go.

I had decided to leave Pru-Bache to set up my own firm. I had hoped the transition would be friction-free, but alas, my exit was anything but smooth. In the end, I had to sue Prudential for spreading false stories and trying to prevent me from recreating my track record. They literally and physically tried to block me from taking my own records out of my department. I convinced my head of research to take them out in his backpack, surreptitiously.

In the meantime, I'd had interest from BNP Paribas (Le Banque de Paris et des Pays-Bas). They asked me to get my track record together as they had an offering for me. So, I recreated the track record based on my purloined records and created what became a very successful fund called the Euro Partners Arbitrage Fund, Limited, a Cayman Islands company, where we had all kinds of investors. They were mostly offshore investors, which included the Kuwaiti Investment Company, but Eastman Kodak also became an investor.

We had lots of grade-A investors, and we grew to about $450 million under investment in that one fund. Although very successful, the more I got into activism, the more it disturbed people. Those investors didn't stay around forever. Kodak stayed until Rusty Olson, who was the manager of their pension fund, retired, then the fellow who took over said, "I don't like activism." So that was the end of that investment, and that happened a number of times. Meanwhile, I won the suit against Prudential, which cost them a million dollars.

And so it was that in February of 1991, at 41 Wall Street—the old Brown Brothers building in downtown Manhattan—I opened up Wyser-Pratte, and my transition from taking over from my father to captain of my own ship was complete. 41 Wall Street was a wonderful place to work from for a number of years until I moved up to Park and 54th Street—410 Park Avenue. There we stayed until about 14 years ago, when I decided I'd had enough of the commuting and moved up to Bedford, New York. But more Wyser-Pratte adventures are to come presently.

On the following page is a chart that shows how my team of 12 employees propped up 12,000 employees of Prudential-Bache for 20 years.

3/8/91   Relationship between Results of Pru-Bache and Arbitr

PERIOD	PRU-BACHE PRE-TAX NET	PERIOD	ARBITRAGE GROSS PROFITS
FY JAN 1969	$20,806,507	(18 MOS) JAN 1969	$5,605,563
FY JAN 1970	(8,344,762)	FY JAN 1970	3,283,250
FY JAN 1971	(6,448,167)	FY JAN 1971	1,893,411
FY JAN 1972	26,337,630	FY JAN 1972	3,171,974
FY JAN 1973	15,611,000	FY JAN 1973	2,672,558
(6 MOS) JULY 31, 1973	(11,500,000)		
FY JULY 1974	(1,873,000)	JAN 1974	2,444,463
FY JULY 1975	17,770,000	JAN 1975	5,233,601
FY JULY 1976	18,976,000	JAN 1976	3,650,542
FY JULY 1977	7,186,000	JAN 1977	5,768,275
FY JULY 1978	8,978,000	JAN 1978	7,118,046
FY JULY 1979	24,494,000	(6 MOS) JULY 1978	4,331,380
FY JULY 1980	47,552,000	JULY 1979	12,076,825
FY JULY 1981	6,041,000	JULY 1980	10,317,645
		JULY 1981	14,761,277
		JULY 1982	3,351,136
FY DEC 1982	(35,396,000)	(5 MOS) DEC 1982	9,686,796
FY DEC 1983	(6,368,000)	FY DEC 1983	15,555,689
FY DEC 1984	(115,262,000)	FY DEC 1984	20,966,201
FY DEC 1985	46,010,000	FY DEC 1985	23,461,595
FY DEC 1986	113,703,000	FY DEC 1986	37,616,098
FY DEC 1987	(127,800,000)	FY DEC 1987	(6,344,328)
FY DEC 1988	80,000,000	FY DEC 1988	114,156,514
FY DEC 1989	(51,000,000)	FY DEC 1989	18,705,248
NET PRU-BACHE PRE-TAX	$69,473,208	GROSS ARBITRAGE PRE-TAX	$319,483,759
		FIXED & VARIABLE	(24,366,000)
		INTEREST *	(92,250,200)
		NET ARBITRAGE	$202,867,559
		NET P-B PRE-TAX	- 69,473,208
		P-B EX ARBITRAGE	$(133,394,351)

* BASED ON 30% EQUITY CAPITAL ALLOCATION

13. THE ACTIVIST AWAKENS

In the book *Merger Masters—Tales of Arbitrage*, the author, famous investor Mario Gabelli, dedicates a whole chapter to me, which I here will summarize to share his perspective. I also encourage reading his full manuscript if you are so inclined. Forgive the respective nature of some of the memories, but it is a macrocosm of the larger story from a second perspective.

Catching the guys at Houston Natural Gas red-handed—that's what really motivated me. Every time I uncovered corporate misbehavior at the expense of shareholders, I felt an immediate surge of purpose. I wasn't built to sit quietly and passively sweat out individual risk arbitrage deals. That just wasn't me. By the 1990s, I was actively going after managements in the United States that were failing their shareholders. The offices of Wyser-Pratte & Co. back then rested in a quiet pocket on the northeastern edge of Westchester County, New York. To reach them, visitors wind through miles of hilly two-lane roads, passing old barns turned art galleries and imposing country estates, until they arrive at Guard Hill Road. A stretch of speed bumps and potholes slows the final approach, leading to a gravel driveway that crosses a narrow gully and skirts a small cottage before reaching the converted red barn tucked into the hillside.

Inside, the office blends rustic charm with financial warfare. A wall of floor-to-ceiling glass overlooks rolling pastures, offering a perfect line of sight for approaching guests. I greet visitors with a straight Marine Corps posture, and I'm always eager to show off the memories—framed mementos, stacks of scrapbooks, and decades of deals. The hum of the trading desk, where a four-person team manages $250 million in assets, is the pulse of Wyser-Pratte & Co.

After attending the University of Rochester on a Naval ROTC scholarship, I was commissioned as a Marine officer. In 1963, I landed in Okinawa with the Third Reconnaissance Battalion. Though I volunteered twice for Vietnam, I never deployed there, leaving active duty in 1966 as a captain. I've always cherished that chapter of my life—the sword, photos, and Marine posters in my office speak for themselves.

Even in the field, my father ensured I kept an eye on Wall Street, having the *Wall Street Journal* mailed to me. After the Marines, I wanted to use the GI Bill for an MBA, but my father had other plans: "Do it at night. Work for me by day." I agreed. My first assignment was to meet his business contacts in Europe. It was glamorous, but short-lived. When my father announced we were merging with Bache & Co., I protested. He threatened to cut off my support. I came home. The 1967 merger gave our arbitrage operation access to larger capital and gave Bache a highly profitable desk. I worked during the day and studied at NYU by night, eventually completing my thesis, Risk Arbitrage, in 1971. The thesis demystified the world of arbitrage, once a closely guarded secret. Passed from hand to hand, it became a cult classic before being formally published in 1982, and later updated in 2009.

Why did I expose the inner workings of the arbitrage world? Partly because no one else had and because my father—brilliant in math—was the best teacher. But also, because I found the industry's secrecy and lack of integrity intolerable. Coming from the Marines, I was used to honor and transparency. Wall Street, by contrast, felt like a snake pit. I almost left. But my father urged me to stay—and I found a way to not only survive but transform the business. I wasn't part of the insider syndicate that swapped confidential tips. I built my own edge—with a sharp floor broker and a determination to avoid the pitfalls of inside information.

Arbitrageurs and dealmakers gained increasing visibility in the 1970s. I found myself featured in a Fortune magazine article in 1977 alongside Ivan Boesky, Bob Rubin, and Dick Rosenthal. Boesky, ever the self-promoter, basked in the spotlight and flooded the industry with new money. Arbitrage spreads shrank, and profitability fell. I began to feel restless.

Eventually, I turned toward activism. I wanted to do more than wait for deals—I wanted to create value. My first taste came in 1974 with Great Western United, owner of Great Western Sugar. After being rebuffed, we sued for unpaid dividends, and the company quickly paid up. I realized then that standing up to corporate management could yield results.

In 1977, I took on Gerber Products. Their board refused a takeover bid, and I sued. We lost in court, but the media attention inspired other activists. I continued the fight—sometimes to the discomfort of Bache's leadership. But I didn't care. Whether it was McGraw-Hill rejecting American Express or any number of entrenched boards ignoring shareholders, I made it my mission to challenge that arrogance. Activist arbitrage became my battlefield. Hostile takeovers, spinoffs, buybacks—whatever it took. The same principles

I learned in the Marines applied: discipline, courage, and a refusal to back down. My approach wasn't always welcomed, but it helped shift the landscape. Shareholders could no longer be ignored.

And I had only just begun.

14. FRIENDLY PERSUASION—A NEW ARROW IN MY QUIVER

Sophie l'Hélias Delattre was Sophie L'Helias when I first met her in the early 1990s. She had been educated in Canada and was a totally bilingual lawyer. Highly intelligent, attractive, tall, and with charm to spare, I heard about her corporate governance prowess from afar. I believe she may have contacted me at some point as she became aware of my own activist initiatives in the United States, but as I figured I was going in the near future to foray into Europe, I should meet her, as she had invited me to Belgium to share matters of mutual interest. She was at that time working for DÉMINOR (an acronym for "defense of minority interests") in Brussels, Belgium. She impressed me from the start at our very first meeting. Soon thereafter, when she saw me publicly agitating around the shares of the French La Redoute S.A., as it had received a ridiculously low takeover offer from Pinault-Printemps S.A., both listed on the Paris Stock Exchange, we spoke about a collaboration to counter this unfortunate attempt to take advantage of minority shareholders, which had for 20 years been my rallying cry. She began to open doors for me in France to get me started with well-known players in the field of corporate governance. First was Mme. Colette Neuville, president of ADAM (Association Pour La Defense D'actionnaires Minoritaires), who agreed to represent my firm and, of course, Sophie. Next was attorney Dominique Schmidt, well-known to both ladies. Then there was the French press. You can't get anywhere without them in France, or for that matter, anywhere in Europe. Of course, the COB (precursor to the AMF) immediately summoned me to size me up, the first of dozens of meetings with the French "gendarme of the Paris Bourse" during the next 40 years of my activities there. Let's just say I was beginning to establish a robust understanding—along with a healthy distrust—of French business ways. This had begun many years earlier as my father purposely placed learning opportunities in my path. Like the time he sent me to Paris to meet Jean Richard of Banque Paris-Bas. My dad had made a small fortune with him on a joint account but rather than acknowledge good fortune such as this, he only dealt with it when escorting me out, when he denied ever making money on the Rendita trade. The Germans have a great expression to connote a guilty conscience: "Butter an kopf," or butter on the head. You can just visualize it melting there.

So, we together decided to sue Pinault-Printemps in the French Commercial Court (Tribunal de Commerce), which was, of course, infested with the aforementioned Freemasons. Schmidt sued under an arcane legal concept known as the "avantage particulier," or special advantage, which the acquirer claimed inured to its benefit as majority shareholder to the detriment of compensation offered to the minority shareholders. This would have been a no-brainer win for us in a US court, but being France, we didn't stand a chance, plus the fact that the president of the COB publicly intervened by taking sides with Pinault (a high-ranking member of the French establishment) and adding publicly that we had no business causing trouble for PINAULT-PRINTEMPS. In response, I publicly reprimanded the COB president for his biased and unfortunate public remarks. My "rude upstart outsider" reputation was thus inaugurated in France, which, over my many years and 38 initiatives there, proved quite valuable. The French investors and public understood very well that I was serious in my purpose and what I wanted to do, which was to help shareholders realize the true value of their shares, and the establishment, well, to say the least, was annoyed. The ghost of dirigiste Finance Minister Jean-Baptiste Colbert (under Louis XIV) still hovered over France.

Corporate governance in France was, in effect, nonexistent at this juncture, until the 1990s. Not only did the La Redoute minority shareholders benefit handsomely from our intervention, but there followed a few years later the Rapport Vienot, an attempt to establish some minimum norms of corporate board behavior, which our public display highlighted as a severe discrepancy with Anglo-Saxon corporate governance. And when this didn't appear to suffice, Daniel Bouton, former Chairman of Banque Société Générale in 2002, scribed a more thorough and far-reaching set of standards for the French securities markets.

In the meantime, Sophie's husband, François Delattre, a smooth and brilliant French diplomat, had been assigned to the Washington, D.C. Embassy as press attaché, an unaccompanied tour. I had attended their wedding in Paris in September 1995 and was duly impressed by such a powerful couple. So, to enable François to take Sophie with him to the States, I engaged her and compensated her accordingly. From that point on, Sophie was stateside, and we worked closely together. First, I sent her to rattle the cages of IPO S.A. (Institut de Participations de l'Ouest) at their annual meeting in 1996, which she did with great success, and to do likewise at the meeting of Siparex shareholders in 1997. She then introduced me to the great French industrialist/corporate raider, Vincent Bolloré, when she saw that both he and I had accumulated sizeable positions in INTERTECHNIQUE S.A. in 1999, enough to attract takeover interest. So, with Sophie as intermediary to avoid legal conflicts, Vincent and I agreed to maneuver the total position into target mode. Smith Industries of the UK soon came knocking, but since the target was a strategic French defense asset (oxygen masks for airplane pilots), the government orchestrated a takeover by Dassault Aviation. Good job, Sophie! There were other triumphs together.

The most humorous of them was when Bolloré asked me to arrange a meeting on his behalf, through Sophie as his intermediary, with none other than Michel David-Weill, Chairman of Lazard Frères, who controlled, among others, La Rue Impériale de Lyon, one of the companies in the Lazard Galaxy. With Michel being quite diminutive and Sophie quite a bit taller than he, Michel decided to invite her to meet at his home office, where he had installed a barber's chair that he could elevate to greet taller guests. So when Sophie entered and Michel gaped at her height, Sophie could discern the whirring of the motor raising the chair so that he became suddenly taller than Sophie. The king, of course, was holding court. She had to restrain herself not to break into historical laughter. Michel never knew Bolloré had sent her to find out the status and intentions of his stock position in Rue Impériale. In fact, Bolloré had built up a large stake in Rue Impériale and wanted to push David-Weill to close the spread between the discounted values of the Lazard chain of companies. David-Weill was obviously frightened enough of the pressure from Sophie and Bolloré that he arranged a merger of the latter with Immobilière Marseillaise, with Bolloré thereby pocketing a nifty $260 million. Subsequently, Vincent and I worked on a few more deals together, such as Groupe Taittinger S.A., Bolloré Group (formerly Papeterie de l'Odet, his family paper company), and even with my nemesis of the last 15 years, Lagardère. Regarding the latter, I went to see him at his office the day before I went public with my proxy battle, asking his advice, "To do (be)or not to do (be), that is the question?" Vincent advised against it, but I was determined. Years later, Vincent surfaced as an interested party in Lagardère and walked away with the prize, whose most coveted asset was Paris Match magazine.

Sophie, unfortunately (for me), had to cool her activist/governance jets when her illustrious husband became French ambassador to Washington in 2011 and Permanent Representative to the United Nations in 2014. Today, she is actively sitting on numerous public and private boards, advising attentive listeners on corporate governance matters. Good for her! She had admirably assisted and propelled me forward in many of my further French endeavors.

The previous examples aren't exactly of the "friendly" variety, but the following tales are of the totally "friendly" type, completely the other side of the coin.

A gentleman named John Wood was one of the earliest allies I had in the European financial world. This was well before Sebastian Freitag—who you will meet shortly—entered the scene, around 1995. At the time, John was working with the merchant bank Kleinwort Benson in London. There was a hostile bid underway: the Trafalgar Group had launched an aggressive takeover attempt of Northern Electric.

The directors of Northern Electric fought back with an unexpected maneuver that threw Trafalgar off course. The British tabloids ran photos of the Northern Electric board popping champagne bottles and celebrating their victory like conquering heroes. The entire London investment community—particularly the old-line British merchant banks like Kleinworts and Morgan Grenfell—was livid. They felt humiliated.

That's when John called me from London. "Hey, Yank," he said, "we need your nice, bright, shiny face over here to help fight these guys."

"Fine," I said, "but I want to understand the situation first."

Once I was briefed, I agreed to go, but on one condition: I wanted proxy authority signed over to me for voting on the issue. John got it done. He rallied his network in the merchant banking world, and they were thrilled to have someone who could act publicly on their behalf—without forcing them to show their own faces.

So I flew out and headed north, all the way to the Scottish border where Northern Electric's headquarters were. I spoke at the company's annual meeting, though I took a bit of a beating—figuratively speaking—from the locals. I believe the term in the area is "barracked." But I made my case. We didn't win that particular fight, but we did force Northern Electric to restructure, and in the end, the shareholders came out ahead.

That was John's doing—he got me involved. He also opened the door to another chapter of my European dealings: the Lazard Galaxy in Paris. That's where I ran headfirst into a conflict with Michel David-Weill over France SA. but more on that in a little while.

John and I recently spoke again. We reminisced about the old days and talked about teaming up once more. We'll see. But that's the story on John Wood—a good man to have in your corner.

Activists/arbitrageurs are experienced and well-positioned to employ their bread-and-butter tactics in offensive, spread-closing operations and are totally, therefore, adept at interpreting the moves, modus operandi, motives, and "Achilles Heels" of acquisitors in advising their target companies on defense.

So, it was that over the years, I was sought out by target companies for my advice on helping them defend against aggressive interlopers.

First was Daniel Bouton, Chairman of Société Générale, who was approached by a raider in March 1999, who turned out to be Banque Nationale de Paris, after Bouton had first arranged to buy Banque de Paris et des Pays-Bas in February of that year. In the middle of this gigantic battle, Bouton rang me up from Paris, soliciting my thoughts and advice. I had never talked to him previously, but he obviously felt confident enough to call me. I told him to play it cool, not get flustered by the aggressive action of BNP's bid for his bank, and to seek the central bank's (Banque de France) intervention. Even though BNP did acquire control of Paribas in this battle, with only 37.5% of Société Générale, the central bank did block BNP from controlling Société Générale. Obviously, too big a bite and anti-competitive for BNP to swallow both banks. The former is healthy, thriving, and independent to this day.

In March 2015, my colleague, good friend, and hedge fund manager Peter Schoenfeld challenged Vivendi S.A., controlled by Vincent Bolloré, to a proxy fight, seeking to duplicate my tactic against Great Western United in 1974 to pay arrears of dividends on their preferred shares. Peter wanted Vivendi to pay a €10 billion special dividend to its shareholders. I spoke to Bolloré and suggested he compromise with Peter, that the latter is a true gentleman and sincerely cares for minority shareholders' interests. Bolloré ended up compromising, paying a special €2 dividend, half in 2016 and the second half in 2017, so roughly €2 billion over two years. A good, well-earned compromise, and peace!

Carl Icahn—a formidable American raider sheltering himself, per usual, behind the clothes of shareholder activism—had accumulated a 13% stake in shares of FedEx Corporation, making lots of his usual noise and blusters about making a run at the company. Fred Smith, a retired US Marine officer, was at the helm and had built a magnificent company serving the entire planet with its on-time deliveries. When this Icahn move was brought to my attention, I called Fred Smith, offering my advice. The Marine Corps is a solid fraternity dating back to its creation by the Continental Congress in 1775, marking its 250th birthday this year. Marines, active or retired, all look out for each other. So, I told Smith to stay very cool. Icahn doesn't have the funds to make a serious run at you. He will tire and fade away if you don't react, which is exactly how it turned out. Icahn sold his shares without further ado, probably at a decent profit, but no takeover! He was probably seeking to "greenmail" FEDEX, which equates to the company buying him out at a premium, which never occurred.

The next iteration of an activist's panoply of roles is an evolutionary one per target, from an aggressive role to a totally cooperative one. Note the following real-life examples:

1. Comsat Corporation (1/13/97–8/9/2000)—We initiated a proxy fight, but luckily, there was a former UofR (my Alma Mater) Board Chairman sitting on Comsat's Board who convinced the President and CEO, Betty Alewine, to meet with me in Washington, D.C. The result was that I was put on the Comsat Board, dropped our proxy fight, and Comsat was sold three years later at a big price to Lockheed Martin.
2. Union Carbide Corporation (3/15/99–12/1/99)—I never took a share position in this one, but I was asked by the Wisconsin Investment Board's general counsel, Kurt Schact, to file a joint provision on the company's proxy statement to require a shareholder vote on any "poison pill" prior to the adoption of said pill. Despite great opposition from the company, we won 52% of the vote so that our provision was adopted, and shortly thereafter Union Carbide received a full merger offer from Dow Chemical Co. Kurt was so taken by our action that he became general counsel of Wyser-Pratte Management Company soon thereafter.
3. Rheinmetall A.G. (12/17/2000–1/28/01)—Soon after taking a large position, we were invited to meet with management. The company was seeking international support in order to raise money via the bond market. Due to our interest from the United States, the shares rose, the company raised the required funds, the shares rose rapidly, and we exited with what the German press labeled "the financial transaction of the year". Since then, the shares have risen roughly 2500% as Rheinmetall has become a leading European defense contractor, making the famous Tiger Tank.
4. Austrian Airlines (5/31/01–3/8/2004)—We were in the process of accumulating a position when the Twin Towers were attacked on 9/11, causing a market rout and a collapse of airline stocks. So, we arranged to fly to

Vienna to meet management in order to render assistance. Managers were thrilled and asked me to be interviewed by their friendly news editors in order to push the airline's employees to reduce their salaries by function: the pilots, the hostesses, machinists, and the like. It worked, with each group taking a pay cut to save the airline from bankruptcy. The airline was saved, and I was given 10 tickets (unavailable to non-Austrians) to attend the Vienna Opera Ball in 2003. My party danced the night away to Strauss waltzes. My mother had always urged me to attend this highlight of the Viennese social season, and she would have been so happy.

5. Vivarte S.A. (Formerly Groupe André) (2/31/99–4/8/04)—Nathaniel Rothschild, of the London Rothschilds, and I had been accumulating shares and, meeting for the first time at the Vivarte Annual Meeting, voted to take over the board, and obtained a majority of board seats. We co-managed the company in a very congenial manner, finally selling it in April 2004 to LBO group PAI Partners.
6. Ingenico S.A. (March 2006–July 2001)—We went public with a 5% position and were quickly invited to join the board of directors. We managed to adopt some key structural changes, allowing me to leave the board in 2001.
7. Prosodie S.A. (3/19/04–3/26/07)—Same as #6.
8. Vossloh A.G. (6/28/06–10/16/06)—One of the most gratifying of all the 101, as it was of a very short duration and a highly successful outcome. We publicized a 3% position while I was vacationing in Cannes. The next day, I received a call from CEO Eichenroder, who asked if he could come talk to me. We arranged to meet in NYC a week later. He asked me what exactly it was I wanted the company to do. I enumerated five steps he needed to take. He flew back to Germany, and a week later, he announced that his company was immediately taking four of the five. The stock roared, and we exited with a smile.
9. Établissements Maurel et Prom S.A. (5/13/07–7/7/08)—I was invited onto this board by Jean-François Hénin, Chairman, and never quite understood why. I think, in retrospect, they were planning to use my presence and reputation as an activist to pursue another company on a hostile basis. So, after a year, I relinquished my board seat.
10. KUKA A.G. (2/3/09–3/25/15)—This was the most hard-fought (2005 proxy battle) and successful initiative of my career. It had started with public accumulations in 2003, which culminated in a proxy fight through which we cashiered management and disposed of most of their unprofitable

businesses. In 2008/2009, my banker and friend Sebastian Freitag managed to attract the Bavarian company Grenzebach A.G. and convinced them to take almost a 25% stake in the company. I then joined the Board in 2009, which held quarterly meetings in Augsburg, Germany. I attended and humbly contributed to the company's emergence as one of the world's leading robotics companies. I left the German Board in 2015, much to the chagrin of board members, shareholders, and local citizens. The local paper featured an article upon my last board meeting: "KUKA will miss its "heuschrecken", or locust, as corporate activists were known in Germany.

So, this activist was perhaps aggressive in style and reputation but was respected in Europe and known as serious and even reasonable.

15. THE MANY FACES OF ACTIVISM

Activism has taken many forms throughout my life—each tailored to the battlefield at hand. Shareholder activism is the one I'm most known for, and it's a powerful instrument for corporate accountability. But there are other forms I've employed just as vigorously. Judicial activism, for example, like my personal letter to the judge in defense of my dear friend Clark Clifford. Political activism—where I've worked to head off policy proposals that would introduce friction or destroy shareholder value. And, at times, geopolitical activism, most recently expressed in an article I wrote condemning the betrayal of America's allies. The article, included below, stands as a fitting example of how I approach activism in its many disciplines.

* * *

THE BETRAYALS OF AMERICA'S ALLIES

What has happened to my adopted country, the United States of America? I was born in France in June 1940. My family and I came here on a troop ship, arriving in New York on St. Patrick's Day in 1946 by way of Ellis Island. We had to escape from France to Switzerland in a rush in 1944 with the Nazis hot on our trail. Coming here in America's "golden age" in the aftermath of the Greatest Generation's rescue of Western civilization, I was enthralled by my new country and became a naturalized citizen along with my entire family in 1952.

I was quickly Americanized, learning English, playing sports, matriculating from the University of Rochester on a US Navy Scholarship, and serving for four years as a commissioned infantry officer in the US MARINE CORPS, from which I left active duty as a captain in June 1966. I felt I had a duty to serve my adopted country that had so welcomed me with open arms. My parents understood my military service, having lived through two world wars in Europe. After all, "freedom is not free."

As I look back to the wonderfully innocent 1950s, I now perceive a repetitive pattern of betrayal of our allies, partners, and friends around the world, and I wonder what happened to the character, moral values, unselfish dedicated public service, and patriotism of the average American. What follows are concrete cases of America failing to uphold its responsibilities to its allies and the alarming loss of nerve to face down its adversaries.

1. THE BAY OF PIGS

The CIA-trained Cuban-exile invasion force (Brigade 2506) landed at the Bay of Pigs on April 17, 1961. They met heavy resistance from Fidel Castro's tanks. A US aircraft carrier was located offshore to provide air cover and close air support to the invaders. President Kennedy didn't have the courage to commit these forces, which would have annihilated Castro's tank forces on the Cuban beaches. The result of this failure was the crushing defeat of the invaders, many of whom were taken prisoner.

As Clark Clifford, a JFK adviser and close friend, confided to me a few years later, he told Kennedy, "Mr. President, you can never do this again!" But this experience served to stiffen Kennedy's spine when he had to confront Khrushchev in the Cuban Missile Crisis. In the end, the United States had to pay for the freedom of the remaining captives in Castro's prisons.

2. SOUTH VIETNAM

Who from that era can ever forget the frightening scene of Americans and Vietnamese running for the ladder to catch a US Marine helicopter atop the American embassy in Saigon on April 29, 1975. The US Congress had been unwilling to further financially support the South Vietnamese military. The North Vietnamese quickly sensed the opportunity, charging down Highway 1 to capture Saigon and subjugating the South Vietnamese population to brutal reprisals.

Thousands fled, some in small boats to the open sea. Many were recaptured. Rather than commit the necessary resources to enable an organized retreat, we simply left those who placed their trust in us to their fates.

3. THE MARSH ARABS

Saddam Hussein drained the lands of the Marsh Arabs (mostly Shia) at the end of the Gulf War, in retaliation for the Shia uprising during the Iran–Iraq War of the 1980s and their support for the US invasion against Saddam Hussein and the entrenched Sunni control of Iraq. The United States, having defeated the Iraqis, looked on and failed to render aid to the Shias despite their pleas. The Marsh Arabs fled to Iran, seeing their lands destroyed.

4. THE KURDS

US abandonment of the Kurdish people has occurred with such an appalling frequency that the relevant instances are too many to highlight individually. The two most egregious of these instances will hopefully serve to illustrate the totality of our betrayal. On March 16, 1988, Saddam Hussein used toxic gas to execute five thousand Iraqi Kurds, the majority of whom were women and children, in Halabja, Iraq.

Despite the Iraqi Kurds tireless commitment to our mutual interests in the region, the United States was content to sit idly by and do nothing. Many years later the Trump administration announced on October 6, 2019, that US troops were withdrawing from northern Syria—not leaving the country, but retreating just enough to leave Kurdish allies defenseless. Turkey unsurprisingly seized this opportunity to invade northern Syria. The Kurdish army had been America's splendid infantry since 2014, and by 2019 had succeeded in defeating ISIS as our proxy army.

Roughly 180,000 people living in northern Syria were displaced, while more than 200 were killed in the ensuing battles. On October 22, a Russia-brokered peace left Turkey and Russia in control of a swath of northern Syria. The United States had allied with the Syrian Kurds while Turkey, itself a US ally through NATO, continued repressing its own Kurdish population while receiving US security assistance. Meanwhile, the United States offered no diplomatic support for the Syrian Kurds. The United States had used Kurdish fighters to beat back ISIS, at great human cost, then left them behind. To cite from a poem by journalist Calvin Trillin, "The Kurds are in the way again, and so we must betray again."

5. THE AFGHANS

The ignominious and precipitous American withdrawal from Kabul Airport in August 2021 was perhaps the low point in American history. Images of desperate Afghans clinging to the wheels of ascending US aircraft are a haunting, eerie reminder of the United States' sudden departure from Saigon in 1975. Hundreds of US civilians were stranded in Afghanistan, and thousands of

Afghans who loyally served American servicemen were abandoned despite promises of US visas for them and their families. Many of these lost their lives at the hands of the Taliban, along with roughly $9 billion of US military equipment and weaponry.

6. MADURO'S VENEZUELAN OPPOSITION

The bus driver–turned President Nicolás Maduro has maneuvered his Supreme Court to block the candidacy of democratically elected Juan Guaidó (President of the National Assembly), who was also recognized by the United States as interim president. Maduro similarly recently blocked the candidacy of Maria Corina Machado after agreeing with the Biden Administration to allow her to run for the presidency. Whereupon Biden sheepishly reinstated some sanctions on Venezuela, but, due to the US political turmoil wrought by the relentless rise in the price of oil, preferred to maintain Venezuelan oil shipments to the United States and forsake Maduro's legitimate position.

Today, the suppression of the Venezuelan peoples' democratic aspirations lingers on as Juan Guaidó has fled and Mrs. Machado bravely stays in Venezuela, having been briefly seized by Maduro's thugs and quickly released due to Trump's pressure. She remains persistently engaged in her effort to force the world to acknowledge the legal voting ballots of the Venezuelan people, which prove the Guaidó majority victory in the July 28, 2024, presidential election. Maduro has been repeatedly asked to disclose his own ballot results, which he is unable to do.

7. UKRAINE?

In a 2024 article in Substack by journalist Timothy Snyder, *The Apocalypse We Choose*, he said, inter alia, that "Ukraine should and can win this war (against Russia). To do so, it needs arms and funds ... Should we fail to assist Ukraine, we will be inviting the worst of catastrophes ... We will put the security of the world at risk ... Americans can enable Ukrainian victory. If we fail to do so, we will face an apocalypse Americans have chosen," and in particular, an apocalypse President Trump has now chosen by hewing to the Putin line that President Zelensky is a corrupt dictator, and that Ukraine started the war with Russia. There is no rational mind that can forget the image of the tank columns surrounding Ukraine on February 22, 2022. Equally indelible is the ignominious speech of Vladimir Putin on the eve of his initiation of the Russian assault, in which he attempted to rewrite the history of Ukraine without mention of the agreements he signed to guarantee Ukraine's sovereignty and independence.

How can we forget Zelensky's retort when asked by Biden if he wanted to be rescued: "I need ammunition, not a ride!" I see striking similarities between today's Republican appeasement of bloody Putin and that of Neville Chamberlain's Munich Agreement, ceding the Sudetenland to Adolf Hitler on September 30, 1938, in exchange for "peace in our time," the tragic assessment of the British Prime Minister. Hitler's blitzkrieg attack subsequently marched into the rest of Czechoslovakia in March 1939 and into Poland in September 1939. Two days later, Britain declared war on Germany. According to no less than Winston Churchill, "Those that fail to learn from history are doomed to repeat it." If we appease Putin now, my apprehension is another world war. Lenin's famous tactic with the West, well ingrained in Russian consciousness: keep pushing your bayonet forward as long as you feel mush. When you hit steel, stop! Putin senses mush in the Republican Trumpers in Congress. Poland and the Baltic States are in his sights!

The least expensive investment that we Americans can make is to support Ukraine with the needed funding for the defense of its democracy. Failing to do so will ultimately cost us more in currency and lost American lives. And of course, Russia, China, North Korea, and Iran, the new Axis of Evil, are watching, along with tinpot dictators like Maduro, who has turned a wealthy democracy into an impoverished nation. The United States has three proxy armies in today's tumultuous world: the Kurds, the Israelis, and the Ukrainians, permitting us to avoid "boots on the ground," protecting our own democratic values and our own blood and treasure in trouble spots around the world. How fortunate are we to have such stalwart peoples fighting our battles for us?

My fellow Americans, get in touch with the values of those who came before us, and for God's sake, stand your ground. It is the history of this great country of ours not to give in to dictators, oppressors, and autocrats. It is a lesson George Washington had to teach to British King George III and one that I hope we can rediscover within ourselves.

* * *

One issue that has deeply troubled me—and spurred the subsequent article—is what's been happening to the US Marine Corps under an initiative called "Design 2030." Now rebranded as "Force Design," it aims to reshape the Marine Corps for future conflicts, focusing on naval expeditionary warfare and so-called Littoral Operations in a Contested Environment (LOCE), along with Expeditionary Advanced Base Operations (EABO). It sounds technical—and it is—but what it amounts to is a dangerous shift in America's first-response force.

General David H. Berger, the Marine Corps Commandant from 2019 until 2023, used the cover of the COVID-19 pandemic to force through sweeping changes to the Corps—changes that would've been unthinkable in the light of day. The Marine Corps has always been America's "911 force," able to respond anywhere in the world on short notice. That capability has rested on the Marine Air-Ground Task Force (MAGTF) structure, an innovation that's served us brilliantly since 1776. General Berger decided to throw that legacy out the window. He dismantled key components of our rapid response ability: scrapping all Marine tanks, eliminating two Osprey tiltrotor squadrons, and disbanding several artillery regiments. Artillery! The very thing we're depending on to support Ukraine against Russian aggression. If you want to know why I find this infuriating, it's because, as I mentioned, I've seen firsthand how essential combined arms operations are. You can't conduct modern warfare without them.

From my position as former Vice-Chairman of the Marine Corps University Foundation, I fought hard to oppose these changes. I joined forces with retired four-star generals, including Generals Jim Conway and Chuck Krulak, both former Commandants and Lt. Gen. Paul Van Riper. Krulak, in particular, was instrumental in publishing the "Marine Corps Compass," a daily bulletin aimed at exposing the damage being done at HQMC (Headquarters US Marine Corps).

We tried everything—pressuring the Corps to host a symposium on Design 2030, persuading the Council on Foreign Relations to investigate, and organizing independent forums to raise awareness. Each effort was quietly squashed—blocked either directly or indirectly by Headquarters Marine Corps. The refusal to allow even a public debate about the direction of our military is chilling.

The concept behind Design 2030 boils down to this: station small missile teams on island chains in the Pacific to deter Chinese naval activity. In theory, it's clever. In practice, it's logistically impossible and politically dangerous. What sovereign nation is going to agree to host US missile units that paint a target on their back? You can't fight a war with no supply lines and no allies willing to share the risk.

It's become such a concern that Congress has finally begun to wake up. They're realizing these changes must be reversed—urgently—before the Chinese make their anticipated move on Taiwan by 2027. Because when the crisis hits, it won't be the academics or theorists who respond. It'll be the Marines. Why? Because they're the only truly integrated ground–sea–air fighting force in the US arsenal. They've got the ships, the infantry, the artillery, and the air wings—three of them: one in Japan, one on the West Coast, and one on the East Coast. They can be anywhere in the world, fast. They're indispensable.

I keep a copy of a 2023 *Wall Street Journal* article with me at all times. The headline reads, "Marine Transformation Spurs Debate." I'd argue it's done more than spur debate—it's sparked a national security crisis. The Congressional Research Service has issued reports asking what the hell is going on.

I've worked closely with former Commandants, intelligence officers, and think tanks to raise the alarm. This is why I engage in geopolitical activism—because I can see what others either don't or won't.

It's not the first time our country has turned its back on its allies. Since 1776, some of our closest and most crucial friends have been the French. Lafayette, Rochambeau—without them, George Washington would never have defeated the British at Yorktown. We returned the favor in World Wars I and II, standing shoulder to shoulder with them on the Somme, in the Argonne, and at Normandy. And the French Foreign Legion returned the favor in freeing Kuwait from Saddam Hussein's murderous grip in Operation Desert Storm.

But in 1954, when the French were surrounded at Dieu Bien Phu in Indochina, President Eisenhower refused to intervene. Two US aircraft carriers were stationed just offshore. Our planes could've easily wiped out the Viet Minh positions, who had surprised the French army by dragging their artillery up impossible terrain, firing downhill on the embattled French. But Eisenhower—brilliant as he was during World War II—held back. The French were slaughtered.

What followed was disaster: the advisory war under Kennedy, Johnson's fabricated Gulf of Tonkin incident, and ultimately, a quagmire in Vietnam. Fifty-eight thousand Americans dead, and three million Vietnamese lost their lives. All because we lacked the foresight, commitment, and—frankly—the guts to act when we should have.

Ho Chi Minh, contrary to popular belief, wasn't originally a communist. He lived in Harlem, New York, he studied American ideals, and at one point proposed a neutral, unified Vietnam. We said no. We chose conflict instead of diplomacy. It took Clark Clifford—with whom I subsequently worked closely—to convince President Johnson that the domino theory didn't hold, as upon being individually queried by Clifford, they didn't care. So, Clark got the bombing of North Vietnam halted. But by then, it was too late. The peace treaty that followed only guaranteed one thing: our strategic failure.

History repeats itself—unless someone sounds the alarm.

That's what I've tried to do. Whether through boardrooms or battlefields, activism has always meant one thing to me: taking a stand when others won't. Not because it's easy—but because it's necessary.

Below, as a clear example of activism, is a letter I penned to Dr. Richard Haass, the then president of the Council on Foreign Relations (CFR) and now president emeritus.

>Dear Richard

I hope you are well and see that you are indeed from your hosting the Prime Minister of Singapore last Wednesday. I have enjoyed all the conferences of CFR over the last two years.

I would like to discuss with you a serious national security issue involving the future structure of "our force in readiness": the United States Marine Corps and its proposed "redesign" according to Force Design 2030. There is a groundswell of opposition to the current Commandant's rushing through the implementation of this project. Many senior officers, both active duty and retired, are concerned with FD 2030 as it relates to our National Security and the role of the Marine Corps in National Security.

As you may have noted from a recent WSJ article by Jim Webb (WSJ 26-27 March edition: "Momentous Changes in the U.S. Marine Corps Deserve Debate"), Webb refers to a group of 22 retired General Officers, including 4 star Marine Generals, former Commandants, Combatant Commanders, Assistant Commandants, and a Chairman of the Joint Chiefs of Staff, who have signed a letter to the current Commandant in opposition to Force Design 2030. Additionally, several recently retired three stars who were in position and offered dissenting views are part of this group.

The attached report of the Congressional Research Service on March 7 raised some serious questions regarding Force Design 2030. The Commandant has already given away a large swath of USMC assets, most notably its tanks, to the U.S. Army. Marines without tanks? Please!

I am in touch with some of these General Officers who have asked me to approach you with a proposal to have a panel of three former Commandants (including a former Chairman of the Joint Chiefs) plus one 4 star firmer Combatant Commander to address the CFR membership on the dangers of this proposed structure to our national security. This panel therefore would be comprised of Gen. Joseph Dunford, Gen. Charles Krulak, Gen. James Conway, and Gen. Tony Zinni. Some of these are CFR members and are well known to you. Some of the similarly inclined senior active-duty Marines will obviously stay in the background.

I am undertaking this initiative for 4 reasons:

1. As a former Marine officer, I am deeply concerned as I see nothing but a one-theater (China) construct which would gravely endanger Marines on a "distributed operations" concept spread out thinly on islands where we are not even sure their presence will be tolerated. The Chinese are closely watching this evolution, I assure you, and are licking their chops.

2. I am a long-standing CFR member and believe we have a duty to inform and advise the oversight committees of the US Congress on such national security measures.

3. I am Vice-Chairman of the Marine Corps University Foundation and am pushing our board to fulfill its fiduciary obligation to our Foundation and to the Marine Corps University, for whom we raise funds and academic chairs. I am asking for an academic review of this project by MCU.

4. Having spent 56 years in the world of finance since leaving active duty in June 1966, I have pursued some 101 corporate governance initiatives against corporations here and abroad and can modestly claim to know a governance failure when I see one. The rushing through of Force Design 2030 under the cover of Covid-19 when the Congress was mostly absent, both in mind and body, is an obvious such failure.

You might remember my intercession years ago in convincing CMC Gen. Hagee to provide himself or the Assistant Commandant for future CFR meetings with the JCS. The US Army had been representing Marines! I also moderated the presentation of Gen. Tony Zinni to the CFR membership during the tenure of Leslie Gelb.

I would like to come visit you about this, Richard to determine how to proceed. I believe time is of the essence, before the list of Marine Corps divestments grows dangerously longer. The list is already remarkable.

The proposed panelists have all agreed to participate and are standing by,

With kind regards,
Guy

* * *

Finally, to round out this chapter on the many faces of activism, my lifetime studying risk is not limited to markets but includes governments, militaries, and the silent negotiations that define the global chessboard. To further demonstrate how to perceive risk, opportunity, and strategy on a geopolitical scale, let's explore what unfolded between Trump, Ukraine, and Russia in early 2025. To my eye, this chain of events was less a blunder than a brilliantly disguised trap. Not that I attribute any of this strategy to Trump personally; he does not possess the manifest intelligence required. And, of course, it is possible that it just went this way, and when he saw the dollar signs from Ukraine and other advantages falling his way, he pounced, as he does at any financial carrot. But let's assume for the moment that this was strategically planned and executed.

It reminded me of 1939—Chamberlain's ill-fated attempt at appeasement—except this time, the result may have been intentional misdirection.

At first glance, the optics were disastrous. President Trump dispatched a new ambassador, Witcof, to Ukraine in February—allegedly to negotiate peace. Instead, Witcof returned grinning from Moscow with nothing but photo ops and a hostage: a symbolic, hollow victory for Putin. The move seemed tone-deaf, especially with 84% of Americans supporting Ukraine and the bulk of Congress—along with much of Trump's own cabinet—united in their defense.

Then came the minerals meeting. On February 28, President Zelensky arrived in Washington expecting to sign a major extraction and reconstruction deal. What he received instead was public humiliation—ambushed politically by Trump and J.D. Vance in what appeared to be a deliberate takedown. Putin was ecstatic. He smelled weakness and believed the West was folding. What followed, however, told a different story.

Witcof made two more trips to Moscow, returning each time with empty ceasefire pledges and trinkets—including, bizarrely, a new oil portrait of Trump. Meanwhile, Russian missiles continued to rain down on Ukrainian civilians. A particularly brutal attack killed 34 people in one strike, even as Putin demanded Kyiv surrender to a laundry list of impossible conditions.

And then the tables turned.

Trump met Zelensky quietly at the Vatican during the Pope's funeral. Days later, the mineral agreement was signed—not on humiliating terms, but with surgical precision: the United States and Ukraine established a joint reconstruction fund, whereby Ukraine would repay the U.S.—not for past aid, but for future weapons deliveries. In a single stroke, Trump shed the burden of prior aid costs (a drum he'd beaten for weeks) while ensuring ongoing arms transfers to Ukraine under a new fiscal framework. The deal was genius in its optics and execution, so obviously there was a real thinker behind it.

Putin, sensing betrayal, erupted. He realized he'd been lured into a war of attrition while the West quietly rearmed Ukraine. The military tide turned swiftly. Within three days, $61 million in F-16 spare parts arrived in Ukraine. Two days later, Kyiv placed a $300 million weapons order. The Czech Republic pledged one million artillery shells. Sweden and Finland added another half-million.

By May, Putin faced the harshest arithmetic of war: an unwinnable, grinding campaign, an exhausted military, and over 800,000 Russian casualties. He had no decisive path forward—only stalemate or retreat. What had seemed like appeasement was, in retrospect, a baited hook.

I respect well-executed strategy. This smelled of General Keith Kellogg—someone who understands theater and force, diplomacy, and deception. It mirrored Reagan's Cold War maneuvering with the SDI "Star Wars" initiative: present the illusion of retreat while engineering overwhelming superiority.

Then came the final stroke—Trump's $150 billion defense budget increase. With one move, he signaled long-term U.S. readiness, deterring China and unnerving Russia. He followed it with billions in arms sales to Saudi Arabia, incentivizing OPEC to increase production. Oil prices dropped 20%. The impact on Russia—whose economy runs on crude—was immediate and brutal. At the same time, the U.S. refilled its strategic petroleum reserve at a discount. That, my friends, is risk arbitrage on a geopolitical scale.

What markets call mispricing, strategy calls misdirection. You don't always show your hand—you let the enemy overplay his. In war, as in finance, the real art lies not in what is seen, but in what is believed. And this, I believe, was one of the most cunning plays I've witnessed in years.

If my assumptions in this narrative are accurate, it's Machiavellian and highly effective—Putin is overextended, under-equipped, and economically strangled. However, this interpretation depends on backroom intelligence and planning we can't independently verify. Still, as a theory of the case, it's coherent, layered, and matches some historical precedent.

16. BROTHERS IN ARMS

GENERAL SHAVENDRA SILVA AND THE BATTLE FOR TRUTH

If you want to understand geopolitical activism—not just deals and boardrooms, but real human stakes—look no further than my friendship with General Shavendra Silva, the former head of the armed forces of Sri Lanka. He and I have always called each other "Bro." That's the kind of bond we share.

Silva commanded the Commando Brigade, the Airborne Brigade—the tip of the spear in Sri Lanka's war against the Tamil Tigers. He held the line when the Tamils broke through to the south, and he saved his country. He became a national hero. We've been close ever since.

He gave me a private tour of Sri Lanka's secret bases. I interviewed his staff at the Sri Lankan War College, trying to understand their outlook—particularly their view of China. It was clear: they didn't want Chinese influence in Sri Lanka. They said, bluntly, "We hate the Chinese. We want the Americans to be our partners here."

And they should be. Look at the map. Sri Lanka is one of the most strategically important pieces of real estate on Earth. It's closer to the Red Sea, the Straits of Malacca, and the Indian Ocean than Taiwan. The sheer volume of global shipping traffic that flows through that corridor makes Sri Lanka indispensable to regional and global security.

When Silva became Sri Lanka's ambassador to the United Nations, we got even closer. I introduced him to everyone I could. I brought him to Marine Corps Headquarters in Washington. To Marine Corps dinners where he met men like Dick Cheney, Justice Scalia, and George W. Bush. We honored him—rightfully.

Silva even lectured at the Marine Corps War College, teaching how his 58th Division outmaneuvered and defeated the Tamil Tigers. His insights became part of the curriculum. But despite his bravery, discipline, and service, a false narrative was being written.

As the war came to an end, the Tamil Tigers turned their artillery on civilians—trying to provoke an international incident. Silva, to his credit, had established civilian safe zones. The Tamils abused them. They launched attacks on hospitals and refugee camps, trying to trigger a humanitarian backlash.

Then came Channel 4—the infamous British broadcaster. They aired a hit piece claiming Silva had ordered the shelling of civilians. It was a total fabrication. There's radar footage showing that the shells came from Tamil positions. I've seen it. But the damage was done. Suddenly, Silva—who had saved thousands of lives and ended a decades-long civil war—was being painted as a war criminal.

I tried everything. I met with the US Embassy in Colombo. I petitioned the CFR. I pushed friends at the State Department. No luck. They had their orders: General Silva was persona non grata.

It infuriated me. Here's a man who set up safe zones. Who played by the rules. Who did everything right. And because of one sloppy piece of propaganda and some diplomatic cowardice, he's been blacklisted. He just recently retired. I called him last week to congratulate him. He said to me, "Bro, can you help me get back to the States? I'd really like to come." I promised I'd try again, and I intend to. Once activism is in your blood, your sense of justice becomes finely attuned and highly resistant to bullshit.

A legal opinion by Sir Geoffrey Nice QC and Rodney Dixon QC reviewed the final stages of the Sri Lankan civil war and found that while the conflict was marked by tragedy, the Sri Lankan military—faced with extraordinary conditions and the LTTE's use of civilians as human shields—did not demonstrate criminal intent in its operations. It provides strong support for the position that General Shavendra Silva acted lawfully under the circumstances. Scan the QR code to review the opinion in full.

Before he joined the military, Silva was a cricket player. He joined the army simply because it was the only way to keep advancing through the cricket ranks. He ended up a four-star general. A true reflection of his commitment. That's the kind of man he is.

He has a beautiful family, enormous discipline, and an unwavering sense of honor. I would vouch for his character morning, noon, and night.

His case is just another example of how geopolitics can crush good men. My fight to clear his name is no different from my own legal battles in France. In both cases, the truth is buried beneath layers of politics, misinformation, and petty revenge. But he doesn't give up. And neither will I.

17. STICKING TO YOUR KNITTING

There's an old saying in business: just because you think you can do something doesn't mean you should. I've learned that the hard way. Especially when cutting my own path, things don't always go as planned—and my foray into the restaurant world was a prime example.

At one point, I decided to get involved with a beautiful little place in Bedford called the Bedford Post. I had always thought it was Richard Gere's restaurant—the actor. It turns out, I was right. Through some contacts, I reached out to his team and said, "Listen, I hear it's not going well. Michael White's group is pulling out and leaving you in the lurch. Why don't you let me step in and run it for a while?"

To my surprise, they agreed. I signed a lease, and off I went into the restaurant business. And let me tell you—there are faster ways to lose a million bucks, but I can't name any off the top of my head.

We pulled out right before COVID hit—pure luck. I managed it for about a year. The place was only half a mile from my house, but every night the staff would walk out with half the restaurant under their arms—ducks, chickens, bottles of wine. I used to say, "Do what you know," and in this case, I didn't know the first thing about restaurants.

So why did I do it? Well ... it was an effort to please an ex-wife. I won't get too deep into that, but there it is.

Richard's wife is Spanish and is a hotelier back in Spain, which I believe was the catalyst for his continuing interest in maintaining ownership. He and I met a few times and decided to go ahead with the idea. But he wouldn't give me a piece of the Bedford Post Inn. That was key. The Bedford Post isn't just a restaurant; it is also a boutique inn—part of the prestigious Relais & Châteaux group. To get that designation, you've got to jump through some serious hoops.

The problem was, unless you own a piece of the inn, there's no money to be made. The location gets no walk-in traffic. It's not like a corner café. Think of Le Manoir aux Quat'Saisons outside of London—a place people take their mistresses to. That's what the Bedford Post is. A very expensive boutique hotel with no casual foot traffic.

About nine months in, I was done. I went to Richard and said, "I'm out." He asked me to hang on and said he needed someone to manage it while he looked for a replacement. I told him I'd give him another couple of months—no rent. He agreed.

Three months later, he came back again. Hat in hand.

"I need more time."

That was it for me. We'd brought in a third-party accountant, who I later discovered was cooking the books—cleaning up the numbers to make things look better than they were. I didn't catch it right away; I didn't have the experience. But eventually, I saw through it. The accountant knew if we realized how bad things were, we'd pull out, and he'd lose the contract. So, he buried expenses, fudged the net cash flow—tried to make a rotten business smell sweet. It was a brutal lesson. Had it not been for my son Jamie, who understood the numbers and warned me every week from his position at my firm's trading desk, "Dad, you're getting ripped off. You are losing $10k per week. Time to get out from under!"

The moral of the story? No good deed goes unpunished. Stick to what you know—stick to your knitting. I had no reservations getting into the business, and no reservations was why I got out.

Still, not all of it was bad. I had a marvelous floor captain—George Thomas. A Jamaican-born former British Army sergeant, wounded three times in Northern Ireland and was even a the personal bodyguard to then-Prince, now King Charles. Built like a tank. Could draw a knife faster than I could draw a pistol. He tried his best to make the restaurant work. He was loyal, efficient, and charming. But no matter how well we ran the place, the people just didn't come in.

And Richard? He could've changed everything with a snap of his fingers. All his Hollywood friends lived nearby. One mention from him would've brought the stars in droves. But that never happened. The only celebrity that was a real friend of the place was Martha Stewart. She came in regularly, always with friends. I knew Martha from when she had her legal troubles. I got her the best criminal lawyers in New York when her best buddy, Charlotte Biers, called me one day, entreating me to get Martha a good lawyer. So I sent her to the Morvillo law firm, one of the best. After a month or so, Charlotte called again, saying Martha needed to make a change, so I called the head of Kaye Scholer, Paul Curran, who had represented me in the past, and Paul agreed to a consultation with Martha. He called afterward to say, "It's too late. She should have come to see me sooner."

Funny thing—she was never convicted of insider trading. What got her was lying to a federal officer. That's what nailed her. But as we now realize, Martha is a survivor and always lands on her feet. She was granted early release and relaunched her businesses across the land. But I think Martha—loyal to those who have supported her—continued to send her friends to my restaurant. Evidently, more was needed to make it a going concern.

Anyway, that was the end of my restaurant career. A million dollars lighter and a bit wiser. I thought I could do better than Michael White's group. When you've been trained like I was, you always think you can do better. And truthfully, I wanted to do something for Bedford. I love this town. When I first moved here in the 1980s, the restaurant at that location was called Nino's. It had great food and a warm atmosphere—everybody came.

But the Bedford Post wasn't set up that way. The model was flawed. They ended up dividing it—one team running the upstairs, another managing the downstairs. Even with the Relais & Châteaux badge on the door, I couldn't make it work. I couldn't stop the theft. I couldn't plug the holes.

I should have known better. And now I do.

18. THE NAME ON THE DOOR—THE RESURRECTION OF WYSER-PRATTE & CO.

New York City, early morning, 1991. The city buzzed below the office windows, but the quiet inside was almost reverent. A single phone. A blank notepad. A nameplate, freshly engraved: Wyser-Pratte & Co.

There's something clarifying about starting over—not just the clean slate, but the fact that everything you build from that point forward carries your name, and your name alone.

I didn't leave a company. I left a structure that had stopped listening. Now it was time to build something that was mine, and I'd live or die by my own wins or mistakes.

The family business had always been arbitrage—that was the legacy I inherited. Back in 1967, E. Wyser & Company was merged into Bache & Company. When I left Prudentia-Bache in 1990, I decided to resurrect my birthright. In 1991, I hung the shingle: Wyser-Pratte & Co.

It wasn't about buildings or furniture. It was about the know-how—the intellectual capital passed down through experience and instinct. That was the franchise. That was the business.

Originally, the firm was E. Weiser & Cie. in Paris, France. It went through iterations, surviving mergers and management changes. But eventually, I reclaimed it under my own name.

After re-establishing the firm, I launched the management company—a Registered Investment Advisor (RIA)—which enabled me to manage funds. But getting it off the ground wasn't easy. I had to extract my track record from Prudential, who refused to release it. So, my research chief, Eric Longmire—my mule—snuck it out, stack by stack, night after night in his backpack.

Eventually, track record in hand, I submitted my proposal to the SEC through a former SEC assistant director, Larry Iason. Once it was approved, I was finally able to sell a fund.

The first fund took off thanks to a Dutchman—an ex-Prudential banker, Job Frowein—who had followed my work. He came to me early in 1991 when hearing of my new beginnings and said, "How would you like to start a fund?" He had international contacts, and he introduced me to heavy hitters: Banque de Paris, BNP Paribas, Newcourt Securities (the London brokerage arm of the British Rothschild family), and Cragnotti Partners in Italy. Together, they underwrote our first fund. It was successful. At first, it was all arbitrage. Later, I leaned into shareholder activism and ran both strategies together in our customer portfolios.

My biggest backer of shareholder activism was Rusty Olson, who managed Eastman Kodak's pension fund. He gave me only one rule: "Just don't get our name in the newspaper." And I never did.

For European success to be possible I needed an international network. I developed a web of connections in Europe which formed the basis of most of my activist initiatives there. Without this network, breaking into the closed societies of Europe would have been practically impossible. It was comprised of the following: Peter Meyer Swantee in Holland, Magnus Matter (introduced to me by Peter), Henri Bouvatier and Pierre Nollet in France, Jean Peterbroeck in Belgium, Sebastian Freitag in Germany, and Robert Blazek in Eastern Europe.

A good example of the effectiveness of this foreign network was when Robert Blazek in Prague invited me to join him in attacking mighty General Foods during their attempt to buy out the minority interest in their subsidiary, Figaro Bratislava, controlled through their Swiss subsidiary, Jacob Suchard. General Foods was subverting Figaro's share price through transfer pricing between Suchard and Figaro in hopes of buying the latter on the cheap. Slovakia had separated from the Czech Republic in 1993, and the illiquid markets were easy enough to manipulate. After meeting with and warning General Foods that we would intervene—and were rudely brushed off—we harassed them by forcibly calling a special meeting of shareholders every month, which we were entitled to do under Slovakian law. This action drove General Foods batty. In the end, the latter surrendered, reversing the transfer pricing and buying out the minority interest at a fair price. We had planted the flag of American capitalism and shareholder rights in a country having just emerged from 70 years of communist dictatorship.

Next, with capital in hand—eventually up to $450 million—I began attacking companies that resisted takeover offers. Sometimes, there wasn't even a bid. De novo, IWKA/KUKA Robots in Germany and Taittinger and Lagardère in France. With Taittinger, we quadrupled the market cap in three years. Claude

Taittinger invited me to his château in Rheims, opened his private cellar, and gave me a remarkable tour during which he asked me, "You know I was with the press corps in the French Army during the attack of the Viet Minh and parachuted into Diên Biên Phủ? "Yes, of course," I responded. "Well, military officer to officer, I would like you to give me the right of first refusal if you ever sell." I said, "Yes, of course." He was a gentleman, and the company was a French crown jewel: Baccarat Crystal, Annick Goutal Perfumes, Société du Louvre, the Hôtel Martinez in Cannes, former headquarters of the Nazis on the Côte d'Azur.

Then came the Sharks. Success breeds attention. My moves on Taittinger attracted French titans like Albert Frère and Vincent Bolloré. Bolloré, a friend, flew to New York and told me, "If the Taittingers don't approve me, accept Albert Frère's offer." He played fair. But behind the scenes, I suspect Frère was maneuvering. Eventually, Bolloré took Lagardère itself—the very company I would later go after. And when I asked him whether I should? He said no. I did it anyway. But as Henry Kravis—redoubtable head of the LBO firm KKR—once remarked to me after having followed me into a Dutch company, "Guy, just keep sending the brides our way." I'm sure I pushed more than one bride into the arms of an acquisitor.

Enter the French Resistance. Lagardère was structured as an SCA—Société en Commandite par Actions. It's an archaic partnership, allowing a small shareholder to control the entire company. Arnaud Lagardère, the heir to his father Jean-Luc's defense conglomerate, with a 9% equity holding, was able to exercise effective control of Lagardère through the partnership structure. I launched a campaign to change that. At one point, I had over 50% support, but the French authorities blocked US votes from being counted. Upon arriving at the shareholders' meeting, I found my company's shares blocked from voting. So, I grabbed the arm of Didier Martin, Lagardère's attorney, and told him to fix it. As a result, I got just 22% of the vote, but I needed 51% of votes cast. I soon discovered all votes in support of my resolutions—mainly to get me on the Board of Directors to dissolve the partnership structure—had similarly been blocked.

I had engaged Dan Burch of Makenzie Partners, a proxy soliciting firm, to get me the vote. Dan is a good and loyal friend and did his best. He assured me of obtaining the US institutional vote, which was substantial. So I asked Dan to collect the actual voting instructions of said institutions, and, sure enough, those votes would have gotten me over the 51%. Even the celebrated US proxy solicitation company ISS (Institutional Shareholder Services) recommended voting for my proposals. This is a key point, as most large institutions subscribe to their input and voting procedures, so when they recommend a plan of action, all subscribers are voted automatically to adhere to their recommendations. As a result, I was going to get 95% of that enormous vote.

Infuriated, I sought the help of the French securities gendarme, the AMF, to investigate. I requested their help three times. The last time, their response was, "Monsieur, we are very satisfied with the result of the Lagardère voting. No investigation is needed. Maybe next year we will have a symposium in Paris to discuss shareholder voting in France!" Democracy, French-style!

Even worse was what followed. My beloved friend, Henri Bouvatier, a former partner at Banque Arjil (The Banque Commanditaire of Lagardère, banker and advisor to the company), who had helped me in my initial foray, constantly pushed me and encouraged me forward: "You must attack Lagardère. I will show you in detail where all the skeletons are located in their closet."

At the Lagardère shareholders' meeting, I got the microphone, as often happens, and had Arnaud Lagardère quite on the defensive. They had planted employees in the audience to pepper me with questions while I spoke. "Why did you leave France to go to the USA," asked one. "I was six years old," I responded with disdain for the irrelevance of the question. And so on it continued with mostly silly questions. Their entire defense was commanded by Ramzi Kirhoun, a former bodyguard and confidant of Jean-Luc Lagardère, who commanded a 30-man team to defeat me. He was Algerian and a former "barbouze"—a hitman for the Corsican police. He was undoubtedly the one who paid off the authorities in the Cayman Islands to force the liquidation of my Euro-Value Fund. But I showed the world I had the goods on these creeps. Arnaud himself was recently forced off of his board of directors and indicted for all sorts of financial malfeasance and faces jail time. The others and I who took up the cudgel were right. Eventually, my friend Vincent Bolloré took control and gained a key gem: *Paris Match* magazine—more on Bolloré later.

A few years after my fireworks at Lagardère, Henri was found in a forest with his head blown off. A suicide note was found. It was ruled a suicide. But I believe he was assassinated. Alain Juillet, the former head of French intelligence (DGE) and Henri's new business partner, confirmed this to a mutual friend. I had worked with Juillet when I was on the board of Ingenico to inform him of money leaving the company for illegal purposes.

It's inconceivable to me that Henri took his own life. He had an incomparable "joie de vivre" and was a great friend. We would call each other every day. I would spend a series of summers vacationing at his beautiful farm in the middle of the Basque Country (Ahetz, near Biarritz). He was happy, after a few failed marriages, to once again find and marry his sweetheart of 25 years prior, when they had met at university. She was Corrina Klasen, the daughter of the former chairman of Deutsche Bank.

Henri was initially introduced to me through a mutual friend to help me out of a stock—Legris Industrie—where I had a 20% position and in which I was quite literally stuck, despite my repeated attacks. When we met the first time for breakfast at the Ritz Hotel in Paris—after chatting for 10 minutes—he asked if we could speak "off the record." "Sure!" He had been told that I was an impossible ogre. "I am stunned," he said with surprise. "You are nothing like you were described to me. You are a gentlemen and a very gentle, kind man."

We became friends on the spot. He got me out of Legris by orchestrating a takeover at a handsome price. He got me out of other tough ones too, like Prosodie. Finally, and fatefully, he pushed me on Lagardère.

I knew he was under pressure from something. He actually wound up in a local hospital with heart palpitations the last time I saw him. What was bothering my poor Henri??

Not long after the initiation of action against Lagardère, the AMF (French SEC) came calling. I was, of all things, accused of insider trading related to Électricité et Eaux de Madagascar (EEM). In truth, I acted only on public information—available through a World Bank release, which I immediately inserted into the Google search engine to determine the involved target, and lo and behold, up popped the name, "Group Viktoria Hotels," the Cambodian subsidiary of EEM. But in France, if they want you, they get you.

I refused to pay the sanctioned €1.3 million. My passport still triggers alerts when I enter France, but my American lawyers confirmed they can't enforce it here in the United States.

I fought the AMF decision through every level—the Court of Appeals, the French Supreme Court, and even the European Court of Human Rights. Nothing! All stonewalled. I eventually brought my case to the European Commission, where I had allies, until a "Smoking gun" letter I had submitted to Tilman Leuder and his EC staff mysteriously vanished, and a key French official—Thierry Breton—intervened. He lobbied—all by his miserable self—to reject a letter of closure agreed to by the head of the Commission's Section DG15, headed by Hugo Bassi, which would have allowed me to reopen the dossier in France and eventually clear my name. Dear scab Thierry was subsequently thrown out of the EC.

I have no doubt this was sabotage. The French judiciary is riddled with Freemasons. Not the moral idealism of Washington's time of highly principled

Freemasonry—but a fraternity of self-serving businessmen. A cape-wearing cult. In the French Tribunal de Commerce, judges are just that: businessmen. When they want to protect one of their own, evidence be damned.

I was tried not on facts, but on whispers. They never called legitimate witnesses and a plethora of documents supporting my actions—only felons and fabrications to choose from. They moved the goalposts constantly in "decisions." One day it was about information timing—alternatively, the supposed "intended" recipients of World Bank announcements—yet another about "intent." The AMF even admitted in an initial decision that professional investors could base their investment decisions on partial information, allowing them to assemble bits and pieces off of the Internet to arrive at even a circumstantial conclusion. That reasoning was simply dismissed when it came to yours truly. Bloomberg, where you get your information as a professional—a very expensive resource where I get most of my information—was considered an insufficient proof of publicly available information. Likewise, the Internet is not public enough where I am concerned. Ludicrous, n'est-ce pas?—is it not? The system was never designed to let someone like me in.

Still, for all the battles, my track record speaks for itself. 101 activist positions over the decades, with an average annual return per position of 38%. That's not luck. That's experience, persistence, and a fair bit of pain.

As I always told people, "If you want to negotiate, I'll negotiate. But if you want to fight, then we fight." My battle strategy was always the same: you put your foot on your opponent's Adam's apple, and when they wave the white flag of surrender, you remove your foot.

I kicked out the chairman of IWKA and turned it into a robotics powerhouse—KUKA. The Chinese eventually bought it out, over my objections. I did everything I could to stop that sale. I went to CFIUS, the Bundeskartellamt, and even Chris Patten's representatives at the EC. No use! The Chinese got the crown jewel.

Now, I'm trying to get it back, if I can, through a process developed and tested by a close friend of mine, Sebastian Freitag.

The short story is: In 2012, German solar module manufacturer SOLARWATT AG underwent a rapid and innovative financial restructuring using Germany's newly introduced ESUG "Schutzschirm" (protective shield) procedure—the first case of its kind. Facing over €90 million in debt, covenant breaches, and a failed consensual recapitalization, SOLARWATT filed for protection under §270b, allowing self-administration and restructuring while still solvent.

The restructuring was led and financed by Stefan Quandt, who increased his ownership from 36% to 94% through a €10 million equity investment. All eight creditor classes—including banks, bondholders, suppliers, and former shareholders—voted in favor of the plan, which included debt deferrals, workforce reduction (23%), and renegotiated supplier contracts.

Bondholders and suppliers accepted a 16% recovery, while banks reopened working capital lines. The process was completed in a record 80 days, demonstrating ESUG's effectiveness in avoiding liquidation and preserving enterprise value. Post-restructuring, the company returned to stability with lower liabilities, fewer employees, and full control under Quandt.

The case is now seen as a benchmark for swift, value-preserving restructurings under the ESUG framework. Essentially, if a company is acquired and the acquirer is or becomes undercapitalized sufficiently to fail the efficient running of the acquisition, the deal can be unwound. I'd like to test the ESUG process with KUKA to see if I can get it out of Chinese control. I just can't let it go. It should never have been put in the hands of our dear friends, the Chinese.

In summary, I've learned a lot through my Wyser-Pratte company journey. I learned that when your name is on the door, it's also on the lawsuit. I also learned the cost and the reward of independence. The company, I am thrilled to say, when I eventually orchestrate my last deal, will go on due to the heir apparent, Jamie Wyser-Pratte, but more about him shortly. Our board-shaking days are by no means behind us. Forced mergers, confrontation of complacency wherever it is found, and activism to bolster shareholder value will be at our core. I didn't build a firm to fit into the industry. I built it to challenge it. I was cutting my own path.

To view Wyser-Pratte returns from corporate governance (shareholder activism) initiatives from 1974 to 2025, scan the QR code below.

19. COURTS, CULTURES, AND CLOSE CALLS

GERMANY OR FRANCE FOR BUSINESS?

The Germans have a very different way of handling their equity culture. There's more of it—more shareholder engagement, more respect for rules of governance. France, on the other hand, has none. That's one of the reasons there were such wild spreads available in the French markets. I did more deals there—37 in all—than anywhere else, especially early on. But it came with a cost.

Activism in France is a minefield. Just take Lagardère. That fight alone brought on a wave of legal and political retaliation. Then came Électricité et Eau de Madagascar—the battle I'm still in today. I hold 20% of that company. It's small but complicated, with overlapping jurisdictional messes involving the French and Cambodian governments, a whole litany of local gangsters, French inhabitants, and corrupt officials.

We've thrown out thugs and grifters. That's why they came after me. I threatened their racket. Germany, by contrast, was a breath of fresh air. I had my run-ins—most notably with Babcock Borsig, a German conglomerate that tried to sell off its crown jewel to One Equity Partners, then presided over by none other than Jamie Dimon, now the redoubtable chairman of JP Morgan in the U.S. My partner in this venture was British Lord Rothschild. We both got fooled. Klaus Lederer, the then chairman, brought false documents to NYC to sollicit our investment. Babcock had filed for the equivalent of bankruptcy-court protection in Germany in July 2002 following the sale of its majority stake in Howaldtswerke Deutsche Werft AG, a German maker of hydrogen fuel-powered submarines and its most profitable unit. The sale terminated a cash-pooling arrangement between Babcock and HDW, in which Babcock used proceeds from HDW to fund its operations. This was the biggest loss of my career.

We won the case in the lower court and then again in the appeals court in Düsseldorf. The German judges—three of them, complete with robes and little square hats—heard the case, deliberated, and sided with us. The rule of law worked. But while the German courts blocked the sale, they put off applying sanctions until they could hold another hearing; in one year, so I had to race back to the United States to try and stop the deal from going through here. That's when I hit a wall: a left-wing judge named Gomez, who let the sale of HDW proceed. Just like that, One Equity Partners acquired HDW, and then made a handsome profit reselling it to German steel giant ThyseenKrupp.

Sebastian Freitag and I had worked hard to find another buyer—Henry Kravis's London office. They understood HDW's strategic importance. But once Gomez let the deal go through, the horse was out of the barn. Still, I always felt well-treated by the German authorities and shareholders. They respected my record—especially from my work with KUKA, Mannesmann, and Rheinmetall, now Germany's largest defense contractor. I told them, "You're a NATO power. Stop hiding behind World War II guilt. You're the primary manufacturer of Leopard tanks. Be proud of it." And they listened.

In France, the attitude was entirely different—hostile, parochial, and clubby. Despite holding a French passport, the establishment and the press—often but not always—treated me like an invading American Marine. One headline read, "American Marine Returns to Raid French Companies."

France is plagued by an institutional rot. The Freemasons dominate the French business courts. It's an old boys' club, cloaked in ceremonial handshakes and closed doors. The Tribunal de Commerce isn't filled with impartial judges—it's businessmen judging other businessmen. If you're not in the club, you're not welcome.

Only at the appellate level do you find real judges. But most activist fights don't make it that far.

I'm currently embroiled in another case in Bordeaux, fighting over a company called Gascogne S.A. The president, Dominique Coutière—a former Socialist Party boss—has rigged the game to drive down the share price and buy out the rest of the company on the cheap. Of course, the court is in his backyard. Imagine my odds.

In 2003, I found myself under house arrest in Paris. The French call it "garde à vue"—police custody. The supposed reason for my detainment was that I had attended a meeting with a partner from Lazard shortly before a takeover was announced. Lazard was the advisor. Their chairman at the time was Michel David-Weill—a powerful man in France, often referred to as its unofficial king.

David-Weill's father and mine had once traded together across the Atlantic. Our families were close. I even hosted a welcoming dinner party for him at the Metropolitan Club in New York City. But that didn't stop him from trying to defraud shareholders through a shady deal involving a group of companies under the Lazard umbrella, particularly France SA.

He even planted a story in the evening paper in Naples so that he could claim he'd already made a public disclosure thereby legitimizing his actions. I sued him.

This was no minor falling out—we were family friends going back to before World War II. Both our families had lived in Cannes. My mother used to point him out as a boy riding his bicycle: "Look, there goes little Michel!"

Michel eventually became chairman of Lazard, largely thanks to his father's reputation—his father was the curator of the Louvre, among other things. My own father had traded with him; they had what was essentially a joint account. When Michel took over Lazard New York, I even hosted his welcome party at the Metropolitan Club. That was no small favor. He asked that women be included—so we invited some of the most beautiful women in New York.

Never got a thank-you.

You had to see Michel to appreciate the scene. He was about 5'2". When Sophie Lelias once visited his office on the Rue Impériale de Lyon, he conducted the meeting from a barber's chair—one he could pump up to appear taller than her. Sophie is a tall woman. It was classic Michel.

Eventually, he paid me a settlement—five million old French francs, under the table. I distributed it evenly to my clients. But he never forgave me. Years later, he saw a chance to hit back.

I was staying at the Ritz in Paris when I received a summons—waiting for me at the front desk. Two days later, I showed up for what I thought was an interview. Instead, they took my shoelaces, my belt, and my tie—and locked me in a cell.

The officer in charge was from Marseille—southern France, more Italian than French. He asked five questions, then leaned in and said, "Can we speak off the record?"

"Yes," I replied.

"I know you're a former U.S. military officer. I was with the French Army."

"Yes, that's correct!"

"So, eh—why are you here?"

"Because my enemies are using your system to get at me."

"You're right," he said, laughing aloud. "Send me everything you have."

I did. I sent him my lawsuit against Michel David-Weill and just like that, the case disappeared. I gave him a small Marine Corps insignia as a token of respect. Of course, it had nearly gone another way. The judge in charge was the infamous Madame de Talancay—an aristocrat, a lesbian communist—France's very own Madame Lafarge, whom Charles Dickens in *Tale of Two Cities* describes as "Knitting while the heads of aristocrats roll into Robbespierre's guillotine basket." Madame de Talencay was known for her zeal and communist politics—just what a conservative like me needed. Fortunately, the police captain left her a generous note: Leave this man alone. He's a professional doing his job.

I walked out of that cell 3 hours later with wings on my feet. I had images of rotting away in a French prison.

Another time, I was pulled out of line at Charles de Gaulle Airport, strip-searched with my wife, and later found out from a well-placed contact that there were standing instructions to harass me at customs. That's France.

The French have a deep inferiority complex when it comes to the United States. They shouldn't. As I've said before, we wouldn't have won the American Revolution without Lafayette and Rochambeau. But that history seems long forgotten in modern France. Germany, by contrast, is confident. Mature. Capable. And much easier to do business in.

One of my favorite German friendships started on a flight—The Concorde, no less. I was reading a German newspaper, covering my Babcock Borsig campaign, when the man next to me suddenly awoke to our takeoff from Heathrow and spilled Coke on my lap. Upon his awaking and after gathering himself, he saw the headline of the German newspaper and said:

"Are you involved in Babcock Borsig?" "Yes." "You must work for Wyser-Pratte?" "I am Wyser-Pratte."

We fast became friends and have been ever since. His name? Sebastian Freitag—a gentleman, a patriot, a banker. When I spoke at shareholder meetings, he'd translate my remarks to German with elegance and precision. He not only won the proxy fight for me against IWKA, by cajoling the UK Focus Fund to vote in our favor. He helped me navigate the active engagement of Johannes Mann, major shareholder, and joining forces with the Bavarian company, Grenzebach A.G., and my eventual ascension to the board of directors from 2009 to 2016. He brought soul to the campaigns we fought together. It's people like him that remind me why I keep doing what I do. Not for the headlines. Not even for the wins. But because, sometimes, you really can make things better—especially birds of a similar feather.

20. FAMILY, LEGACY, AND THE SOFT SIDE OF A STREET FIGHTER

There's only one part of my life I've always kept mostly private—my personal relationships. In my current life, I'm blessed. I have a wonderful wife, three beautiful children, and five incredible grandchildren. I don't dwell on the past marriages. Frankly, it's not a pretty picture, as you witnessed in the knife-wielding drug-master scientologist chapter. But that, too, was part of the journey.

If I'm honest, I have always had a soft spot for women in trouble—something I trace back to my relationship with my mother. That shaped a pattern in me: the rescuer. But here's the thing about being a rescuer—it turns you into a facilitator. And facilitators, well, they don't fix problems. They prolong them. I made that mistake more than once.

It took me years—and a few scars—to understand that you can't rescue anyone but yourself. Firemen, Marines, priests, policemen—we all share that impulse. But if you live by it in your personal life, you become a target. As my son once told me, "Dad, you've always had a target on your back."

Twenty years ago, I met my wife, the love of my life, Cristina. We dated, but I didn't realize at the time how significant it was. When I took her around Manhattan Island for my birthday on a private yacht and threw her a dinner party with everything just so, in hindsight, that wasn't just a celebration—it was a signal. But I didn't act. I got distracted. Made a mistake. I married someone else.

Eventually, I came to my senses, and Cristina has been the grounding force in my personal life ever since. But let me tell you about this near miss.

SANTA MARIA CRISTINA—LIFE BEGINS AT 80

Sometimes life gives you a second shot at something you should never have let go. In my case, that something—or rather, someone—was Cristina.

We first met over 20 years ago at my daughter Joëlle's birthday party. There was an instant connection. We dated. It was good—until I made a wrong turn.

Literally and figuratively. Life, pride, timing—call it what you will—I lost her. And I carried that regret for years.

Fast forward to 2020. The world was upside down, and so was I. I went to see Joëlle and told her, "I'm miserable." Without missing a beat, she looked at me and said, "I'm your daughter. You don't think I know?" Then she asked the most important question: "What are you going to do about it?"

I didn't hesitate. "The biggest mistake I ever made was Cristina." She didn't respond right away. She just nodded, and then when I left, she quietly picked up the phone. She called Cristina. Arranged a dinner. The twist? Neither of us knew we were coming to see each other. Joëlle had engineered the whole thing.

The first attempt didn't quite go as planned. I was out in the Pennsylvania countryside, about 200 miles away in my Porsche. Joëlle called, "Get back here. Cristina's coming." It was 8 PM. I hit the highway like a bat out of hell—only to run over debris and flatten not one, but two tires. Trip over. No one drives a Porsche on two flats. Joëlle kept calling. "Where are you?" "On the highway, waiting for the crash truck."

Evidently, I missed the dinner. But Joëlle wasn't giving up. She tried again. And this time, it worked. When I walked into her house and saw Cristina, I didn't say a word at first. Then, in Portuguese, I looked at her and said:

"Santa Maria Cristina."

She smiled.

Cristina—full name Maria Cristina—was still the same woman who'd once captivated me, maybe even more so. We picked up where we left off, except this time I had no intention of letting her go. We're back together, happily married, and at the time of this writing, we're heading to her old home, Brazil.

* * *

One of the other great joys in life is raising children. Especially when they're young. They're like warm muffins out of the oven—pure joy. I have pictures of my oldest riding on my back as I mowed the lawn. Simple stuff, but golden.

I used to play catch with my son in the backyard. We called it "a nice friendly game of catch"—where we'd hurl the ball at each other as hard as we could. One time, my pitch went over his glove and nailed him right in the forehead. It wasn't great. But moments like those stay with you. We can't all be the father of the year every year. It's all part of the process.

Today, that son works with me. He's the future of the firm. He picks things up fast—faster than I did from my own father. He doesn't have an MBA, but he doesn't need one. He called me one day to say he'd quit his PR job and was looking for another. He's already gone out to two other PR firms. I said, "Do you really want to be in PR for the rest of your life?" He said, "No! I want to come and work with you." I said, "That's a given. Come aboard. About time!" He's been thriving ever since.

We considered sending him to business school. I did mine at night while working. But frankly, it's not worth it anymore. The market moves too fast; the lessons on the ground are more valuable than any textbook.

An MBA is part theory, part basic math and accounting—you can pick all that up on the job. Theoretical economics is often wrong anyway. What matters is knowing how to read the market in real time. I always say, "When the ducks are quacking, feed them." If the crowd is rushing in, sell. There is an old adage: "When the butcher, the baker, and the candlestick maker are all at the gold window to buy, it's time to sell." Because eventually, there won't be anyone left to buy.

The one driving purpose for educational credentials is not the education itself but the fact that you need it to get a job. If you already have a job, and can work for yourself and survive, you will get more than any education they can give you at a learning institution.

For five years, I had a Marine major—a field-grade officer—work at the firm for a one-year stint. It was part of a special program championed by General Chip Gregson, who also got me into the CFR. The Marines wanted to learn how we evaluate risk in the corporate world, and I couldn't think of a better setting than arbitrage and activism. You're always under fire.

Those Marines brought discipline and insight. We gave them exposure to fast-paced decision-making in high-stakes environments. It was a mutual exchange—and one I cherished.

Eventually, the program was cut due to budget issues. But the relationships lasted. Chip Gregson became a trustee of our foundation. He fought hard to get me on the Council, even when they tried to keep me out for being too outspoken, too unorthodox. Eventually, they gave in. Now I am a lifetime member of the Council on Foreign Relations. Even so, just as when I tried to raise alarms about the disastrous restructuring of the Marine Corps, they gave me lip service and moved on. That didn't stop me. I pushed. I wrote letters. I pulled in generals. But the system, as usual, resisted.

In summary, family is foundational to me. My family is spread around the world and continues to grow. I'll continue to advocate for each of them in any way I can, whether it's one of my children, grandchildren, or a faraway friend—family is everything.

Of course, all families have battle scars and skeletons. I recall at the age of 13, walking into my parents' bedroom and there, for the world to see, was a rather large, framed photo of a German SS officer with red armband swastika et al. "Who is that?" I asked my mother. "That's your uncle Tony," she replied. To which I commented, "Well, I can never bring my friends in here to see that."

Tony went through the trials at Nuremberg after the war, was acquitted, and eventually became District Attorney of Graz, the family home town. When he developed stomach cancer, my mother inveighed upon my father to pay for his surgery, which he did, of course. So, in the end, the Jew paid to save the Nazi.

21. MY REMAINING SUMMERS

Eventually, I suppose I will have to eject from the cockpit, roll my last trade, file my last suit, and smoke my last cigar—as must we all. Before I leave my post and march on up that highway, I have some thoughts to share about my time here and what I'd like to do with the summers I have left.

My number one thing that I want you to take away from this book, if nothing else, is my driving ambition to finish what I start and to leave it all better than I found it. That's my quintessential understanding of legacy. If all we leave behind is some money, who will we really impact?

For me, it's my family and hopefully what I have built into them. It's my son, continuing the work. It's those backyard baseball games, those early mistakes turned into life lessons. It's the Marines who passed through our doors and left with sharper instincts. It's a career built not only on deals and proxy fights, but on people—those who stick, those who matter.

It's the quiet pride of knowing you didn't just fight for companies—you fought for your name. And you didn't go down easy.

The four years I spent in the Marines were the best four years I ever had, full of adventure and opportunity. Imagine for a moment, a young kid of 22, suddenly becoming a second lieutenant. All the responsibility put on your shoulders that you can possibly handle. As a platoon commander, I was responsible for 30—I call them young hoods. Half of them were there by choice, and the other half were given a choice: either go to prison or join the Marines. So they chose the latter. I had people from Brooklyn. I had farm boys from Indiana under my command. They were from every walk of life. It was really an experience. I had to meld these guys into a unit. It was truly quite something.

The Marines give you tough training. You really have to carve something out of these blocks of granite. It stood me in good stead as a businessman, an arbitrageur, an activist, and a father.

But we don't all get to serve in the military. And if you're not serving in the military, I think everyone owes it to themselves and others to serve in some kind of humanitarian outfit. An NGO, a refugee mission—something. I ended up doing exactly that. I served for several years with the International Rescue Committee (IRC). And let me tell you how I got roped into it by a Norwegian superstar.

It all started, as these things often do, at a gala dinner. They sat me next to Liv Ullmann, the legendary actress and humanitarian. We struck up a conversation, and at some point, I decided to tell her a story. I don't know what possessed me, but I started talking about this play I'd once seen in London—August Strindberg's "Miss Julie." Now, what I didn't realize when I walked in, suited up and ready for a fine evening of theater, was that the whole thing was in Swedish. Yes, Swedish. In London.

Of course, by the time the fire doors closed—this being a proper British theater—there was no escape. So I sat through the whole damn thing trying to piece it together from gestures and dramatic tone. I think I got the general idea, but not much else.

When I told this story to Liv Ullmann—who, let's not forget, is the queen of Nordic drama—she laughed so hard, she was practically on the floor. I thought I'd made a fool of myself, but she found it hysterical. We bonded, and by dessert, I'd been recruited by the IRC. Liv wasn't just charming; she was persuasive. I joined up, and not long after, I was on a plane to Cambodia, which was still simmering from the Khmer Rouge years. This was up in the north—Battambang and the Patumbang province—and we were checking in on refugee resettlement zones.

The Khmer Rouge was still skulking in the bush at the time, and I remember thinking, "If I don't catch a bullet here, I'll count this trip as a success." These guys were ruthless, remnants of Pol Pot's regime, and they had no love for outsiders.

Luckily, I spoke French—and so did many of the Cambodians, thanks to the old colonial legacy. That helped. But the country was teetering. The refugee villages were fragile, aid was scarce, and behind the scenes, Hun Sen was rising to power. He did what I feared: consolidated control, blocked out every other party, and replaced potential leaders with intimidation, payoffs, and old-school strong-arm tactics.

But the mission itself—seeing these communities survive in spite of it all—was rewarding. It gave me another channel for that drive I've always had: to fix things, to help people, even in places where it seems hopeless.

That evening with Liv Ullmann turned out to be more than just a good story. It led to one of the most meaningful chapters of my life. I joined an organization I respected, saw parts of the world most people never do, and helped—if only a little—to rebuild after devastation.

So yes, Swedish tragedies aside, unlikely events conspired to open a door into something far more important: se. My years exercising my "watcher muscles" left my radar wide open to opportunities. Willingness to serve will always allow opportunities to manifest, and that has been one of the great blessings of my life. My father taught me how to pay attention to the details, to see the small signals, and to be open to what things are trying to tell you.

If I can teach as many people as possible to do the same, to step up and act, to do what is right, then that is my legacy. Even through this book, perhaps my voice will be heard, and others will be influenced to influence. The world needs activists. Don't sweat the money. Do what's right, and the money will come. And for crying out loud—Cut Your Own Path.

LETTER TO MY YOUNGER SELF—EPILOGUE

Dear Young Guy,

You'll spend your life running toward the fire. It's in your blood. Maybe it started the moment you crawled back through that hole in the fence, curious about the sound of hoofbeats and too young to know better. You'll outrun Nazis, wrestle Wall Street, stare down corrupt boardrooms, and—on occasion—bare your heart to the wrong woman. You'll live fast, speak truth, and sometimes burn bridges you didn't mean to. That's okay.

Because here's what I can tell you, looking back from the summit:

Courage isn't the absence of fear—it's the decision to press forward, knowing full well the cost. And you'll pay it. In scars, in solitude, in sacrifices that no one sees but that define you more than success ever will.

There will be times you'll feel like the only one who sees the cliff edge when others are still dancing on it. Trust your instincts. They'll serve you better than any diploma or business card. But temper them with kindness. Because power without compassion is just another form of cowardice.

You'll try to do what's right in a world that rarely rewards it. You'll lose friends, make enemies, and challenge empires. Good. That means you stood for something.

But don't forget the quiet victories: teaching a junior banker the value of courage, mentoring a Marine, protecting your children, honoring your parents. Those moments matter more than headlines ever will.

If there's one lesson I wish I'd learned earlier, it's this: the most valuable asset you'll ever hold isn't a stock or a strategy. It's time. Spend it with intention. Not just chasing greatness, but enjoying the little things—baguettes with your dad, glances with your mom, the feel of cold rink air on your face, a Sunday dinner that ends in laughter. That's the real wealth.

And one more thing—keep your damned windows closed in a storm.

Yours in reflection,
The Older Guy.

La fin

Institutional Investor
MAY 1992

Why it's not smart to rile Guy Wyser-Pratte

Some companies just bring out the shareholder activist in an investor. So Cleveland-based container and machinery maker Van Dorn Co. learned to its chagrin last January when it rashly proclaimed that it wasn't for sale and rejected a takeover bid by competing container company Crown Cork & Seal. And when the incensed shareholder activist happens to be Guy Wyser-Pratte, watch out. The former Pru-Bache arb, who has run his own investment shop since 1990, bought 3 percent of Van Dorn's shares after Crown announced its $18-a-share (soon raised to $20) offer. After Van Dorn rebuffed the bid and fortified its takeover defenses, its share price dropped from $19 to the mid-teens. (Wyser-Pratte had bought his stake at an average of $18 a share.)

"There is no such thing as 'This company is not for sale at any price,'" fumes the ace arb. So Wyser-Pratte is thrusting himself into the takeover battle. "We decided to lead the charge," he says. "We're doing this more for honor than for money." Urging

shareholders to reject management's directors slate at May 1 annual meeting, Wyser-Pratte in late April was hop that dissident nominees wo win and then cow the board i dismantling Van Dorn's b wark of takeover barriers that fails, he — along w another Van Dorn stockhol investment firm Spear, Leeds Kellogg, whose reputation a pit bull makes it a good ally face-off — plans to soli shareholder support to com Van Dorn to call a special m ing to allow a vote on the b ers. If Wyser-Pratte preva fur, and bids, could fly. Ne theless, Van Dorn CFO Thom Miklich, while concerned, s management will win ov "regular shareholders who h more long-term value." Who er wins, Wyser-Pratte, who not exactly a docile investo Pru, has made shareholc activism that much more acti

Shareholder Wyser-Pratte: The nerve of some companies

Investors in France and Germany have found their voice, writes Jason Corcoran

Votes mark breakthrough for shareholder power

Wyser-Pratte: led rebellion at Germany's IWKA that led to the resignation of its chief executive

«Rambo» til angrep på Tandberg-toppen

Scan the code to view the related image gallery in full color or visit www.CuttingMyOwnPath.com

www.ingramcontent.com/pod-product-compliance
Lightning Source LLC
Chambersburg PA
CBHW032101150426
43194CB00006B/605